Easy Guide to
Sewing Linings

Connie Long

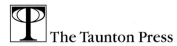

The Taunton Press

Cover photo: Jack Deutsch

Book publisher: Jim Childs
Acquisitions editor: Jolynn Gower
Publishing coordinator: Sarah Coe
Editor: Diane Sinitsky
Indexer: Nancy Bloomer
Designer: Lynne Phillips
Layout artist: Susan Fazekas
Photographers: Jack Deutsch, Scott Phillips
Illustrator: Christine Erikson
Typeface: Goudy
Paper: 70-lb. Somerset Matte
Printer: R. R. Donnelley, Willard, Ohio

Taunton
BOOKS & VIDEOS
for fellow enthusiasts

Printed in the United States of America
10 9 8 7 6 5 4 3 2 1

The Taunton Press, Inc., 63 South Main Street,
P.O. Box 5506, Newtown, CT 06470-5506
e-mail: tp@taunton.com

Library of Congress Cataloging-in-Publication Data

Long, Connie.
    Easy guide to sewing linings / Connie Long.
        p.   cm. — (Sewing companion library)
    Includes index.
    ISBN 1-56158-225-5
    1. Linings (Sewing). 2. Underlinings (Clothing). I. Title.
II. Series.
    TT557.L66   1998
    646.4—DC21   97-47113
                                                      CIP

To my husband, Ron, for your help, support, and patience. You are the best!

To my parents, Giovanna and Tino, for encouraging my interest in fashion and sewing at an early age.

And to my friends, colleagues, and students at G Street Fabrics for making it such a great place to teach.

EASY GUIDE TO SEWING LININGS

Introduction

I consider adding a lining the ultimate way to clean-finish any garment I sew. A lined garment does not cling, is more comfortable to wear, is easier to slide on and off, and looks just as good on the inside as it does on the outside. Adding a lining to a dress or skirt eliminates the need to wear a slip. Lining even the simplest style improves the garment's finished effect and is an important ingredient in sewing clothing that rivals high-quality ready-to-wear.

This book will give you the information you need to complete beautiful lined garments and to reline garments you already own. Once you master the basics of lining, you'll want to make the lining an integral part of the total design and even something to show off. You can do this by selecting lining fabrics that complement or contrast rather than match the fashion fabric. Or you can use a splashy or whimsical print to line a sedate style, or play up a highly textured fashion fabric with a smooth satin lining.

The first chapter discusses the purpose of lining a garment, the types of linings that are appropriate for particular garments, and the principal elements of lining. You will learn to decide which qualities are important in choosing a lining fabric, whether it is durability, wrinkle resistance, weight, or luxury. You will be able to distinguish lining from underlining and to understand the best application for each. Since there are many lining alternatives to choose from, you will learn to select the method that is aesthetically pleasing to you, is compatible with your skill level, and suits the amount of time you have to sew.

Subsequent chapters are organized by garment type, with one chapter devoted to lining sheer and lace garments. Since most commercial patterns do not include a lining pattern, you will learn how to make your own. Then you will learn to sew and insert linings by following detailed instructions. Whenever possible, both traditional and quick methods for constructing and inserting linings are included. Finally, you will learn how to line the vent area of any garment.

1 The Purpose of Lining a Garment

A lining is a functional and luxurious finishing touch to a garment. Although it's not always visible, it improves the overall quality of anything you sew. There are practical and aesthetic reasons to line any garment, but the primary reason is to cover the inside layers. Lined garments not only look better but they also feel better and are more comfortable to wear. They slide on and off easily and wrinkle less than unlined garments. The lining also takes some wear and strain off of areas of stress. Adding a full lining eliminates the need for most seam finishes and ultimately saves time. A lining added to dresses, skirts, and pants is the easiest way to create a smooth, flattering silhouette.

Just because a lining is useful and functional does not mean that it needs to be boring (see the photos on p. 4 of some of the linings I have used in jackets). Since coat, jacket, and vest linings will be seen by others, using contrasting colors, jacquard fabric weaves, and prints add interest to the overall style. The fabric you select gives you the opportunity to enliven and personalize the design and create your own signature look.

In this chapter, I'll discuss the different types of garment linings and how to choose the best lining fabric for your garment. I'll show you how to prepare the lining fabric for sewing, then how to adjust a basic pattern for cutting the lining. Finally, I'll talk about considerations when lining asymmetrical garments, pocket linings, lining to the edge, and finishing seams and hems.

Unusual and luxurious linings make the finished garment more interesting.

A full jacket lining completely covers the inside seams of a garment.

Types of Garment Linings

The most common lining is a full lining, which usually appears in jackets, coats, skirts, pants, and dresses. However, there are many varieties of partial linings and underlinings that perform some of the same functions as a full lining.

Full lining

A full lining completely covers the inside seams of a garment and gives a garment the most finished look. You can fully line any type of garment, but a full lining is especially useful on coats, jackets, and any garments that have interfacing layers, inside pockets, and other inside construction details to cover. You may attach the lining by connecting all of its edges to the garment as in a jacket or vest or attach it so that it is free hanging. A free-hanging lining is connected to the garment at the neckline, facings, or waistline but is hemmed separately from the garment. This is useful on dresses, skirts, and pants because it is simpler to install and makes pressing the garment easier.

A partial lining covers the part of the garment that benefits the most.

airy. Or you can line the body and not the sleeves on a sheath so the body of the dress does not cling. Unlined sleeves are cooler and less restrictive to wear. Skirts can be lined just above the back vent or only in the back panel to control stretching in the seat.

Pants can be partially lined to the knees both in front and back, only in the front, or only at the knees depending on the fabric you are using. When you line the pants front and back to the knee, you derive the benefits of a full lining. The pants look fully lined as far as the eye can see when you look into them from the top, and they slide on and off easily. Lining just the front to the knee helps to smooth the smile creases at the top of each leg and keeps the knee area from stretching.

Partial lining

Partial linings cover only the parts of the garment that benefit the most, while the rest of the garment is left unlined. This is a good option if you want to keep a garment lightweight. For example, you can line just the bodice on a dress with a full skirt to clean-finish the bodice edges and cover the construction details. Leaving the skirt unlined keeps the dress lightweight and

Underlining

An underlining is a layer of lightweight fabric that is treated as if it is one layer with the fashion fabric. You may underline the entire garment or just a part of it. Underlining adds body to the fashion fabric, helps the style keep its shape, and makes the fashion fabric less transparent. Underlining can also be used to stabilize loosely woven fabric, especially at the seams, and to prevent the fashion fabric from stretching or wrinkling. You can also use underlining to prevent seams and other construction details from showing through to the outside when sewing with sheer, semitransparent, or light-colored fabrics of any thickness.

Although lining and underlining are not interchangeable, you can combine the benefits of both by using a lining fabric to underline the garment and to finish the seam edges as well. The resulting garment then has stable seams, keeps its shape, and looks neat and well finished on the inside. This method works well on simple skirts (see pp. 83-85) or pants (see pp. 104-105).

If you need to underline the fashion fabric but plan to line it as well, lightweight fusible interfacing can be used as the underlining layer. Using fusible interfacing is easier and faster than sewing in the underlining layer and then sewing the lining.

Underlining is a layer of lightweight fabric that helps to support the fashion fabric.

Choosing Lining Fabrics

Selecting the best lining for your project is easy once you set your priorities based on what qualities are important to you—durability, wrinkle resistance, washability, luxuriousness, being lightweight, or adding warmth. Then you can select the fabric that best meets your standards.

Every fabric store has a variety of fabrics made exclusively as linings, but you will find more interesting options if you look at blouse and dress fabrics as well. Lining fabrics come in a range of weights from lightweight, such as China silk, to heavyweight, such as flannel-backed satin. The fiber content may be rayon, polyester, acetate, nylon, cotton, or silk.

Many different fabrics can be used for lining.

other layers of fabric. A slippery lining is a disadvantage when lining strapless dresses and bodices that require boning. These dresses stay up due to the boning and the close-to-the-body fit, but slippery linings would cause the dresses to slide down, no matter how tightly you fit them.

Linings made from natural fibers and rayon breathe but are likely to wrinkle. Linings made of polyester or nylon are washable and don't wrinkle but can feel clammy in hot, humid weather. A cotton lining is not slippery, but it breathes and feels cool to wear, making it nice to use in summer dresses, skirts, and pants. Acetate lining comes in a variety of weights and weaves, but it is my least favorite lining because it frays easily, especially on close-fitting garments. I think it's a good choice if you need an inexpensive lining for a garment that is not worn frequently, such as a prom dress or a costume. A silk lining is comfortable to wear because it is absorbent. It feels cool in the summer and warm in the winter. Silk fabric dyes beautifully so the color and luster are unsurpassed.

You will also find a selection of fabric types or weaves, such as sheath lining, satin, twill, taffeta, crepe, faille, jacquard, batiste, and broadcloth. Whichever lining fabric you choose, it must be compatible in care and maintenance with the fashion fabric.

With a few exceptions, the lining should be smooth, tightly woven, and nontransparent. Most lining fabrics are slippery. This is an advantage most of the time because the slippery lining easily glides over the body or

My favorite linings from the dress and blouse fabric section include silk and polyester crepe de Chine, charmeuse, and jacquard weaves. Solid or printed, these make luxurious linings for jackets and coats. Also consider using cloth made out of microfiber, which has a luxurious feel and drape and is very tightly woven. Rayon or polyester faille and rayon jacquard weaves also can be used to line outerwear. Polyester taffeta, either plain or with a moiré finish, makes a wonderful tightly woven, crisp lining (so does silk taffeta but there is a huge difference in price). Silk, polyester, or rayon chiffon and georgette can be used to line chiffon, cut velvet, or lace garments. Silk or polyester organza makes a beautiful crisp, sheer lining for a crisp lace fabric or can be used to self-line an organza garment.

Sometimes garments require unusual lining fabrics. Sheer and opaque tricot knits, lightweight rayon knits, and lightweight swimsuit linings also serve to line soft, drapey, woven fashion fabrics, bias-cut garments, and fashion fabrics that stretch.

My lining requirements vary depending on the type of garment and how it will be worn. For example, my highest priority in selecting a lining for skirts, pants, and dresses is wrinkle resistance. By now you probably think my wardrobe is full of polyester double knits but the opposite is true—I sew almost exclusively with natural fibers. But since most natural fibers wrinkle, I like to line skirts, pants, and dresses with a polyester sheath lining that is antistatic. Doing this creates a smooth foundation and helps to cut down on outside wrinkles in the fashion fabric. When lining jackets or coats, wrinkling is not an issue. Here I look for a tightly woven durable lining that is attractive enough to wear on the outside. You don't have to use the same lining fabric for the entire outfit. When I sew a suit, I may use a glorious silk jacquard lining in the jacket and a functional polyester sheath lining in the skirt, pants, or dress that completes the outfit.

A word about using expensive blouse fabrics as linings if you're on a budget: When you find a fabulous but expensive lining, use it to line the body of the garment only and purchase a standard lining for the sleeves.

Preparing the Lining Fabric for Sewing

To prepare the lining fabric, it must be preshrunk just like the garment fabric. Before beginning to sew, it is also important to choose the proper markers, thread, and needles.

Preshrinking

Lining fabrics for washable garments must also be washable. With the exception of polyester, which does not shrink, it is necessary to preshrink the lining fabric using the same care methods you will be using on the finished garment. If you are making a dry-clean-only garment, you can steam most linings by using the lowest steam setting of the iron. If I'm using a silk or rayon lining in a dry-clean-only garment, I preshrink the lining fabric the same way I preshrink blouseweight and dressweight silks. I wet the silk or rayon lining before cutting to reduce the water spotting that can occur during sewing if water gets on the fabric. For this reason, preshrinking is a good idea when the fabric washes well. If the fabric doesn't wash well, doesn't look as good after wetting a sample, or you don't like the change in texture that could occur in silk or rayon, just use steam.

If you're going to preshrink without simply using steam, wash your silk in a cool water bath, starting with a small swatch first to check for running or bleeding color. If the color runs, add ¼ cup to ½ cup of white vinegar to the water. Do not let the fabric soak; gently move it around in the solution, then rinse in cool water. Without wringing the fabric, lay it on towels, roll it up, and blot it dry. Iron the fabric with a dry iron while it is still quite damp, pressing in a lengthwise direction. To speed up drying, you can also use the tumble dryer on a fluff (no heat) setting.

Choosing markers

Powder pencils or air-erasable markers are best for marking dots and other matchpoints on lining fabric, while wax-free or air-erasable dressmaker carbon is best to mark lines and darts. Avoid waxy markers because they will stain lining fabrics that have a silky finish. Try to do as much marking as possible by using scissor snips. For example, to mark the dots along the curve of the sleeve cap and the armscye, simply take shorts snips along the cut edge with the tips of the scissors.

Selecting thread and needles

Lining fabrics come in a variety of fibers, weights, and finishes. All-purpose 100% polyester thread is appropriate for all lining fabrics. Cotton-covered polyester thread and 100% cotton thread should only be used on linings made from natural fibers or rayon.

Select a universal-point needle, in a size ranging from 9 to 12, for most lining fabrics. You should use the finest needle that works on the fabric (the lower the size number the finer the needle). To choose a needle, start with a size 9 or 10 needle and sew on the lining fabric. Look for pulls in the fabric to each side of the needle. Sometimes called railroading, these pulls are normally caused by using a needle that is too large or damaged. If your fabric gets pulls, try a finer needle size. If the finer size needle still causes pulls, try switching from a universal-point to a sharp-point needle, particularly for very tightly woven fabrics such as taffeta and very thin fabrics such as China silk. China silk is so thin and lightweight that I usually sew it using an extra-fine sharp-point needle and extra-fine thread. In this case, I would use size 8 sharps or Microtex needles with either silk size A thread or fine, size 60 two-ply cotton machine-embroidery thread.

Making a Lining from the Garment Pattern

You can add a lining to any style garment, whether it's simple or complex, by modifying the basic pattern pieces. It's easy once you understand the relationship between the garment, the facings, and the lining. In the classic lining application, the facings and hems finish the outer edges of a garment, while the lining connects to the facings and covers the remaining body of the garment. On skirts and pants with waistbands, the lining connects to the waist seam and is enclosed by the waistband. Lining to the edge is another way to line nontailored garments such as dresses, skirts, and pants

with waist facings and vests. This method eliminates the facings and connects the lining directly to the garment.

Adjusting the basic garment pattern for cutting the lining may require making allowances for the facings, adding a vertical pleat or a horizontal pleat called a jump hem, or simply changing the length. Adding a vertical center back pleat to jacket and coat linings ensures that there is enough ease across the back for movement. The jump hem adds lengthwise ease and prevents the lining from pulling up and distorting the bottom and sleeve hems. In most cases, you can make adjustments for cutting the lining directly on the garment pattern or on the fashion fabric. You should always press the garment and facing patterns before marking in the lining cutting lines so you can accurately measure and line things up.

Creating a lining pattern for a garment with facings is easy once you understand the basic principles. On the finished garment, the lining connects to the innermost edge of the facings with a ⅝-in. seam allowance. In other words, the lining begins where the facings end. To make a lining pattern, subtract the width and shape of the facing from the garment pattern it finishes and add seam allowances so you can sew them together. For example, position the front facing pattern underneath the front garment pattern, lining up the outer edges. You should see the inner facing edge through the pattern tissue. The inner facing edge is the reference point for adjusting the pattern because this is where you connect the lining. The lining must go ⅝ in. past the facing edge just to reach the sewing line, and it needs an additional ⅝-in. seam allowance for sewing that becomes the cutting line. So you would mark the cutting line 1¼ in. from the facing edge and toward the outer edge of the garment. This is how you make the allowance for all types of facings. Other specific adjustments are included in the appropriate chapter for each type of garment.

Cut out the lining on the same grain as the garment. The best length to cut the lining is equal to the length of the finished garment plus a ⅝-in. seam allowance. This length works when sewing a connected hem by hand or machine and when sewing a free-hanging hem. To avoid cutting up the garment pattern when you cut the lining, first cut all outside seams, then run a tracing wheel with or without carbon to mark any changes to the front and neck edges onto the lining fabric. Remove the pattern and cut on the marked line.

When you add a back pleat, mark the center back for about 2 in. at the neck, waist, and hem on the fabric. Transfer any other pattern markings such as darts, pleats, and matchpoints. Vertical darts can be changed to pleats in the lining by marking the widest part of the dart for about 2 in. into the lining. To sew, bring the lines together, stitch, and press to one side.

Sewing Techniques with Lining Fabrics

Most lining fabrics are slippery, so you'll need more pins when aligning lining pieces than you would if aligning fashion fabric pieces. When constructing the lining, adjust the cut edges between pins as you sew each seam to keep them lined up. If you are sewing lining seams that are on grain, keep the fabric taut so you will have a smooth seam. Pull the fabric firmly in front of and behind the presser foot and move with the same pace as the machine. Let off-grain areas feed under the presser foot normally and sew directionally. Run your finger along the fabric's cut edge and sew in the direction that pushes the fibers toward the cloth. Doing this controls stretching.

When connecting the lining to the garment, position the more stable fabric on top and place the layer with the most ease on the bottom. Which layer is more stable depends on the combination of fabrics you are using and on the part of the garment you are sewing. For example, when attaching a skirt lining to a skirt at the waist seam, sew with the lining on top if the skirt appears slightly bigger and has to be eased to match the lining's matchpoints. On the other hand, if the lining needs to be eased into the skirt, sew with the skirt on top to prevent the presser foot from pushing the ease forward and misaligning the matchpoints.

Use a machine baste stitch to sew the lining hem to the garment hem. A stitch length of 4mm or 5mm will not strain the seam and is easily removed should an adjustment be necessary.

Lining Considerations

In most cases, I have included the instructions for making a lining pattern within the chapter for a particular garment. What follows is information about linings and lining techniques that can be applied to many different garments.

Asymmetrical linings

Be sure to cut and sew the lining for an asymmetrical garment so that it is the opposite of the garment. When using the garment pattern to cut the lining, cut with the pattern wrong side up and the fabric right side up to facilitate marking. If your lining fabric is the same on both sides, be sure to make the bottom the wrong side. Mark darts by placing dressmaker carbon under the cut-out lining with the marking side facing up. If your pattern only has notches, mark the wrong side of the lining with a powder fabric marker or tape.

Pocket linings

Although the fabric used to line the rest of the garment is serviceable as the pocket lining, pocketing material provides better results when sewing welt, slanted, and in-seam pockets. Pocketing material, found in the lining section of your fabric store, is usually a twill-weave cotton or poly/cotton fabric. The color selection is limited to neutrals, but this doesn't matter because you won't see the inside pocket. If you prefer, you can also use a cotton or poly/cotton broadcloth, either of which comes in a wider range of colors.

Inside pockets made with a cotton fabric are more durable and easier to install. Welt pockets lined with cotton fabric hold their shape better. Crisp cotton fabric helps keep double welts from drooping open.

Patch pockets, flaps, and in-seam pockets can be self-lined if the fashion fabric is very thin. If not, these can be lined with the same lining as the rest of the garment or a lightweight, slippery lining. You can greatly improve your results when sewing patch pockets and flaps by doing a few simple things. If you choose to use interfacing, which will make a pocket smoother, use the lightest weight, all-bias fusible interfacing for the pockets and flaps no matter what interfacing you use for the rest of the garment. The lightweight interfacing cushions the outside layer without making it stiff and inelastic. If a fusible interfacing is not compatible with the fashion fabric, you may be able to fuse the interfacing lightly and for the least amount of time it takes to hold it in place without harming the fashion fabric. It's a good idea to do a test fuse first to make sure you are not flattening or damaging the fashion fabric.

Cut the lining layer with the lengthwise grain going across the pocket or flap (see the illustrations below and on the facing page). If the fashion fabric is thick, trim 1/8 in. from the sides and bottom of the pocket and flap linings to allow for turn of cloth and keep the lining seam tucked under. When you connect the pocket and flap to their linings, sew with the lining layer on top and keep the edges aligned. If necessary, baste before sewing. The resulting pockets and flaps curve gently toward the back side because the lengthwise grain is very stable.

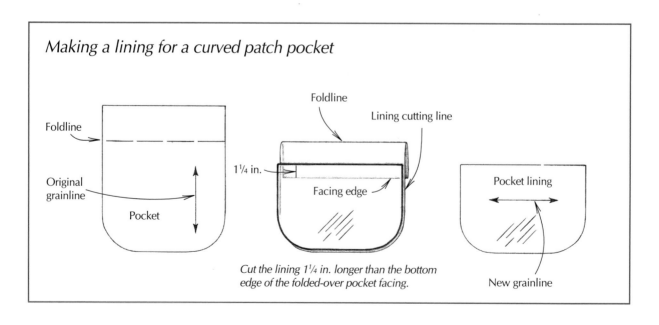

Making a lining for a curved patch pocket

Foldline

Original grainline

Pocket

Foldline

Lining cutting line

1¼ in.

Facing edge

Cut the lining 1¼ in. longer than the bottom edge of the folded-over pocket facing.

Pocket lining

New grainline

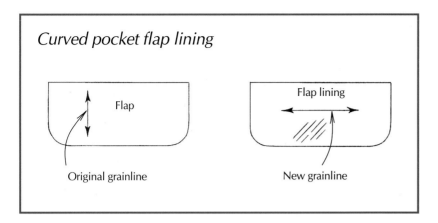

Curved pocket flap lining

Flap

Original grainline

Flap lining

New grainline

Lining to the edge

When using fabrics on which facings are best eliminated, lining garments to the edge is a good idea. These fabrics include scratchy or very thick fabrics such as metallic brocade, quilted or embossed fabrics, sheer fabrics, sequined fabrics, and lace. This lining application is the simplest way to add a lining to the garment, working especially well when hemming the garment and lining separately or when free hanging the lining. When lining to the edge, the lining is cut the same as the fashion fabric.

Vests are frequently lined to the edge without allowing for a back pleat or a jump hem. For best results, the vest fabric and the lining fabric should be very compatible. For example, lining a soft or stretchy outside fabric with a rigid lining opens the door to all kinds of pulling and distortions.

When lining a simple jacket to the edge, add a center back pleat and jump hem to the lining to prevent pulling during wear. Lined-to-the-edge garments can also be made reversible, which is most common on simple jackets, vests, and sleeveless tops. Lightweight or sheer tops are often self-lined in the same or contrasting color.

Finishing seams

Seams and hem edges can be left unfinished as long as they will be completely enclosed and the fabric does not fray. If the fabric is loosely woven or frays easily, you should pink, straight-stitch, zigzag stitch, over-the-edge stitch, or overlock stitch the garment edges. You need only do the minimum amount of work necessary to prevent fraying. Once the seams are enclosed, they will stay neat.

If you will be using a free-hanging lining, use a zigzag stitch, over-the-edge stitch, or

A variety of methods can be used to finish seams, such as an overlock stitch (top), straight stitch and narrow zigzag (bottom right), and a French seam (bottom left).

overlock stitch to finish garment seams that ravel. Keeping the lining seams together where possible, double-stitch the seams using a straight stitch and a narrow zigzag stitch or an overlock stitch, or sew together using a French seam.

Finishing hems

There are many hem finishes you can use for your garment. Choose the one that is right for the fabric and style.

Zigzag, over-the-edge, or overlock stitch Finish the edge of the garment hem using a zigzag stitch, over-the-edge stitch, or overlock stitch. Zigzag and over-the-edge stitches work best on medium to heavy fabric hems that are on grain or slightly

curved. Over-the-edge stitches, also known as sewing-machine overlock stitches, vary slightly from machine to machine. Using an over-the-edge foot, or overlock foot, prevents the stitches from distorting the edge. The serger overlock stitch works on fabrics of all weights and can be used on straight or circular hems. Sew the hem using a catchstitch (see the illustration on the facing page) or a machine blindstitch.

Rayon seam binding or lace edging The hem can also be finished by machine-sewing rayon seam binding or lace trim on top of the hem edge, overlapping the ends at a seam. Rayon seam binding and lace edging cover up the raw edges so you don't have to use an additional edge finish. They don't add any bulk and they can be used on all types of fabrics. You can shape the rayon seam binding using a steam iron to follow moderate curves. When using binding, sew close to the lower binding edge, then fold back the binding and sew the hem using a catchstitch.

Hong Kong finish The Hong Kong finish is an elegant seam finish, where bias-cut fabric wraps around the raw edges of the seam or hem. This finish is good for medium to heavy fabrics, especially ones that are loosely woven or fray easily such as Chanel-type tweeds. You can use a bias 1¼-in.-wide lining

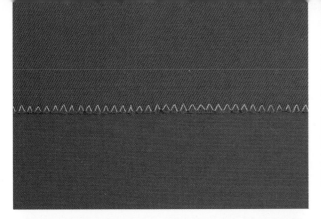

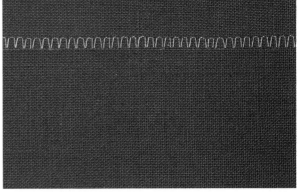

Hems can be finished using a zigzag stitch (above left), over-the-edge stitch (above right), and overlock stitch (left).

Catchstitching a hem

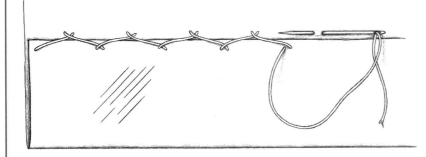

To use a catchstitch, sew from left to right with the needle pointing to the left. Using single thread, hide the knot on the wrong side of the hem and bring the needle and thread through the hem edge. Take a small stitch in the garment fabric above the hem edge and 3/8 in. to 1/2 in. to the right. Take the next stitch the same distance away but in the hem. Continue alternating stitches.

Lace edging can be used as a hem finish.

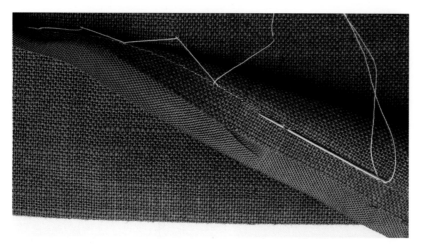

You can use rayon seam binding as a hem finish, then a blind catchstitch to hem the garment.

You can use a Hong Kong finish as a hem finish, then a blind catchstitch to hem the garment.

fabric, 1¼-in.-wide packaged bias tricot, or net. Stitch to the right side of the hem edge using a ¼-in. seam allowance, then wrap the binding around the hem edge and stitch from the right side in the well of the seam. Sew the hem using a blind catchstitch.

Turning hem under and slipstitching Finish the edge by turning the hem edge under ¼ in. and using an uneven slipstitch to sew the hem (see the illustration on the facing page). This technique is good for thin fabrics.

Turning hem under and topstitching Finish the edge by turning the hem edge under ¼ in. and topstitching close to the fold. This technique is recommended on sporty top-stitched garments. Use a narrow turned and stitched hem when the garment or the lining flares at the hem.

Lining hem The lining hem should be 1 in. shorter than the garment. Turn back the lining hem twice to equal the total hem allowance. For example, if the hem allowance is 3 in., press the hem back 1½ in. twice, then topstitch close to the upper crease.

Lining hem using lace trim With the right side of the lace trim and the lining facing up, position the lace on top of the lining so that the lower edge is

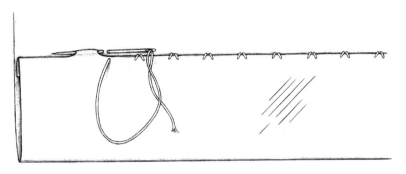
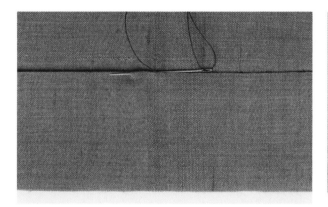

Turning the hem under and slipstitching works well for thin fabrics.

Turning the hem under and topstitching is good for sporty garments. On flared hems, use a narrow turned and stitched hem on the garment and lining layers.

1 in. shorter than the finished garment length. Pin and sew close to the upper edge of the lace using a straight stitch. Trim the lining behind the lace, leaving a ¹⁄₄-in. seam allowance, then press the seam allowance away from the lace. With the lace facing up, stitch again on top of the straight stitch using a zigzag stitch setting of 2mm for the width and length.

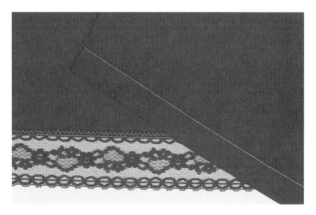

For the lining hem, turn the hem under twice and topstitch, or sew lace to the edge of the lining for a decorative touch.

2 Jacket Linings

I like to select luxurious or whimsical lining fabrics for my jackets. My favorite fabrics for lining jackets are not from the linings section of the fabric store. They are silk or polyester, crepe de Chine, charmeuse, jacquards, and faille. Blouseweight fabrics made from microfibers are densely woven and durable. Rayon crepes are also nice to use because they have a soft drape and are available in trendy prints. Most of these fabrics are available in a variety of interesting prints and in a sandwashed finish that creates a sueded effect. What these fabrics have in common is their silky drape and feel. Crepe de Chine is at the top of my list because it has a subtle sheen that complements most fashion fabrics and a texture that makes it slightly elastic and resistant to wrinkles. Charmeuse has a high sheen that makes it more susceptible to snagging, but it contrasts beautifully with a textured fashion fabric. Jacquard fabrics have woven surface designs and make interesting linings. These jacket linings feel wonderful next to the body and are meant to be seen.

Other appropriate fabrics from the linings section are China silk, rayon sheath lining (also called Bemberg), polyester sheath lining, cotton batiste, cotton broadcloth, and various acetate twills, dobies, and satins.

When shopping for the lining fabric, it's a good idea to have more than one fabric in mind. Your first choice may not be the best match or the most complementary to your fashion fabric. I often wait until the jacket is in its final stages of completion before selecting the lining. By doing this, the lining not only matches the fashion fabric but also captures the flavor of the total design.

In this chapter, I'll show you how to adjust a jacket lining pattern and how to make your own full and partial lining patterns if one is not provided. Then I'll discuss how to construct and insert both full and partial linings. Finally, I'll tell you how to add underarm shields.

Adjusting a Jacket Lining Pattern

Even when the lining pattern is provided, there is often an inadequate hem allowance. To check for a sufficient hem allowance, compare the finished length of the jacket to the finished length of the lining by overlapping the back pattern pieces. Line up the center back and shoulder seam. If you subtract the hem allowances, usually 2 in. on the jacket and ⅝ in. on the lining, the two pattern pieces should be the same length. If the lining cutting line does not fall ½ in. or ⅝ in. below the finished jacket hem, lengthen all the lining pieces by the desired amount.

When adding a lining to an unlined jacket pattern, be sure the jacket hem allowance is 2 in. wide. A 2-in. hem gives the best results when connecting the lining hem to the garment hem.

Making a Full Lining Pattern

Most classic and designer jacket patterns provide a lining pattern. If not, the following instructions will show you how to make your own pattern. The first step is to create a back neck facing when one is not included with the pattern.

If one lining pattern from a particular pattern company doesn't need adjustment, don't assume that will be the case with other patterns from that company. I've checked several patterns from the same company and some had adequate hem allowance while others did not.

Back neck facing

I like adding a back neck facing for several reasons. Without a facing, the back neck area of the lining is the first part of the lining to show wear. Also, it is easier to machine-sew the lining pieces when there is a facing. A back neck facing is essential if you are going to install the lining completely by machine using the bagged lining technique, the name of which comes from the bag that is formed during the process of sewing the hems together and turning the jacket right side out (see pp. 37-39).

To create a pattern for the back neck facing, place some pattern tissue on top of the back pattern and copy the neckline curve and shoulder seam. Eliminate the center back seam allowance if there is one, and draw a line at the center back for cutting on the fold. Then measure the width of the front facing along the shoulder seam. Make the back neck facing the same width around the neckline (see the illustration at left on the facing page).

Jacket body

To create a pattern for the jacket lining, mark changes for cutting the lining directly on the main pattern pieces. Begin by positioning the front facing pattern under the front pattern, matching the outer edges and notches. The inner edge of the front facing is the reference for cutting the lining. The lining will need ⅝ in. to reach the sewing line along the facing and ⅝ in. more as a seam allowance. Thus, draw the lining cutting line 1¼ in. from the inner facing edge, nearer to the front edge. Use a sewing gauge to draw the curved sections of this line, and mark "lining cutting line" on your garment pattern. Mark the cutting length of the lining to be the same as the finished jacket length plus ⅝ in. Lower the front

and back shoulder at the armhole by half the thickness of the shoulder pad, then taper to the original line near the neck (see the illustration below right).

Position the back neck facing pattern under the jacket back pattern. When the jacket has a center back seam, the jacket pattern will need to extend ⅝ in. past the facing pattern at the center back. Draw the lining cutting line 1¼ in. inside the facing edge. Mark the lining

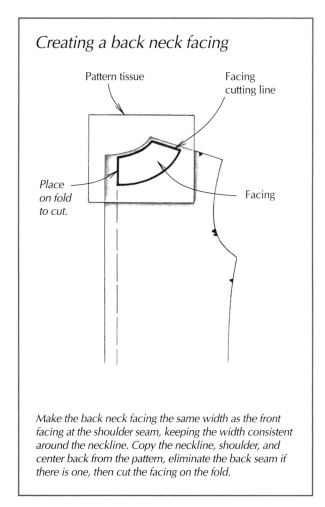

Creating a back neck facing

Pattern tissue

Facing cutting line

Place on fold to cut.

Facing

Make the back neck facing the same width as the front facing at the shoulder seam, keeping the width consistent around the neckline. Copy the neckline, shoulder, and center back from the pattern, eliminate the back seam if there is one, then cut the facing on the fold.

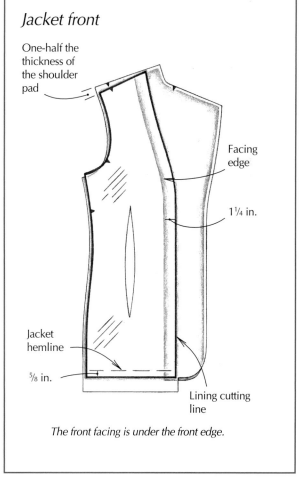

Jacket front

One-half the thickness of the shoulder pad

Facing edge

1¼ in.

Jacket hemline

⅝ in.

Lining cutting line

The front facing is under the front edge.

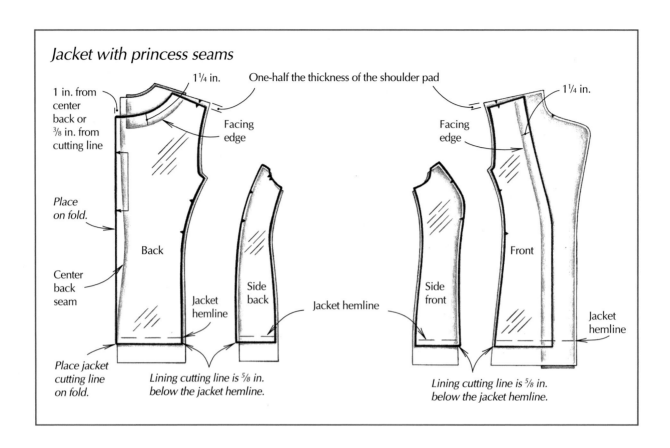

Jacket with princess seams

1¼ in.

One-half the thickness of the shoulder pad

1 in. from center back or ⅜ in. from cutting line

Facing edge

Facing edge

1¼ in.

Place on fold.

Back

Front

Side back

Center back seam

Jacket hemline

Side front

Jacket hemline

Jacket hemline

Place jacket cutting line on fold.

Lining cutting line is ⅝ in. below the jacket hemline.

Lining cutting line is ⅝ in. below the jacket hemline.

length ⅝ in. longer than the finished jacket length, then add a center back pleat using one of the methods on pp. 25-26.

To create a lining pattern for a jacket with princess seams, place the front facing pattern under the front pattern, aligning the outer edges. Mark the lining cutting line 1¼ in. beyond the inner edge of the front facing, then lower the slope of the shoulder near the armhole by one-half the thickness of the shoulder pad (see the illustration above). Next, mark the lining cutting line ⅝ in. below the

finished jacket length. Use the side front pattern to cut the side front lining and the side back pattern to cut the side back lining, altering the length only so the cutting line is ⅝ in. below the finished jacket length. Changes to the back are the same as for the standard back.

If you are making a shawl-collar jacket, which has no back neck facing, place the front pattern on top of the front facing pattern, matching notches, and mark the lining cutting line 1¼ in. beyond the facing's inner edge (see the illustration on the facing page).

Next, mark the cutting length ⁵⁄₈ in. below the jacket's finished length. Lower the front and back shoulder at the armhole by one-half the thickness of the shoulder pad, then blend to the original line near the neck. When cutting the lining, add a center back pleat according to the type of back seam you have on the jacket.

Center back pleat

A center back pleat ensures there is enough ease across the shoulders and allows for differences in the garment layers. Add a center back pleat using one of the following three methods.

Straight center back Use a straight center pleat when you cut the lining if the jacket back is cut on the fold or has a straight center back seam. Add a 1-in. pleat by placing the center back 1 in. in from the fabric fold. (When there is a center back seam, place the center back cutting line ³⁄₈ in. from the fabric fold.) Moving the pattern 1 in. from the fabric fold adds 2 in. of fabric to the center back lining (see the illustration at left on p. 26).

Shaped center back Cutting the shaped center back on the fold eliminates the back seam,

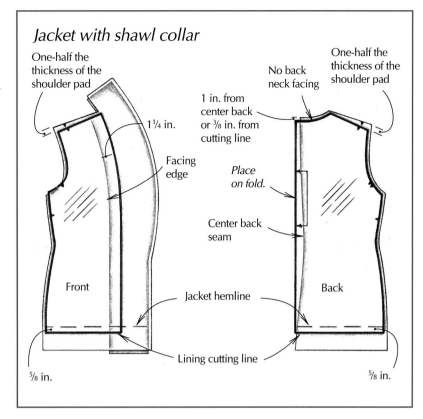

Jacket with shawl collar

One-half the thickness of the shoulder pad

1¼ in.

Facing edge

Front

Jacket hemline

Lining cutting line

⁵⁄₈ in.

No back neck facing

One-half the thickness of the shoulder pad

1 in. from center back or ³⁄₈ in. from cutting line

Place on fold.

Center back seam

Back

⁵⁄₈ in.

making the sewing neater, faster, and easier. Place the center back 1 in. from the fold of the fabric at the neck (the cutting line is ³⁄₈ in. away), and place the cutting line on the fold at the hem (see the illustration at right on p. 26). This results in a center pleat with widths of 1 in. at the neck and ⁵⁄₈ in. at the hem. The width at the waist, where the pleat will be widest, will vary with each pattern depending on the shape of the back seam.

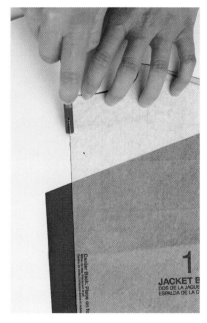

Mark the center back pleat.

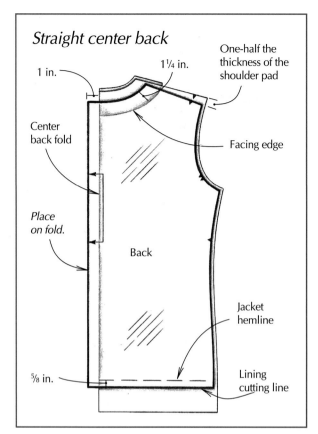

Straight center back

1 in.

1¼ in.

One-half the thickness of the shoulder pad

Center back fold

Facing edge

Place on fold.

Back

Jacket hemline

⅝ in.

Lining cutting line

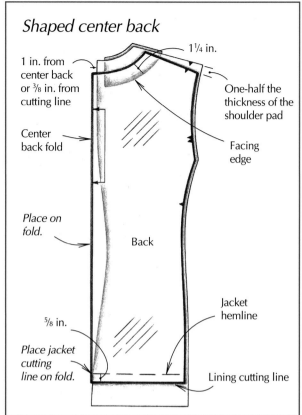

Shaped center back

1¼ in.

1 in. from center back or ⅜ in. from cutting line

One-half the thickness of the shoulder pad

Center back fold

Facing edge

Place on fold.

Back

⅝ in.

Place jacket cutting line on fold.

Jacket hemline

Lining cutting line

When the jacket pattern includes a lining pattern, eliminate the back seam and change the pleat. Pattern companies add the back pleat only above the waist. I like to continue the pleat to the bottom because a narrow pleat is better than no pleat at all. Continuing the pleat to the bottom eliminates any strain that might occur and allows for adjustments should they be needed. To change the pleat, use the lining pattern and angle it along the fold of the fabric so the pleat is 1 in. wide at the top and ⅝ in. wide at the hem.

Straight or shaped center back with a vent Linings for vented seams must also have a seam. Add 1 in. to the center back at the neckline and taper to the ⅝-in. seam just above the vent (see the illustration at top left on the facing page). For more on vents, see Chapter 10.

Sleeve

To make a sleeve pattern, reduce the sleeve cap by the full thickness of the shoulder pad and raise the underarm ½ in., tapering both to the original lines near the notches (see the

Center back with vent

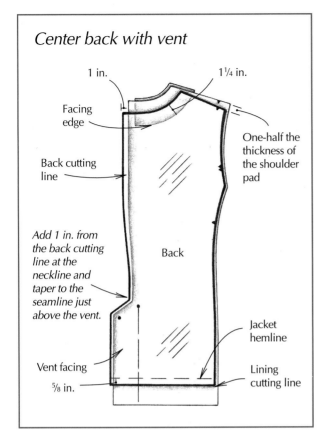

1 in.

1¼ in.

Facing edge

Back cutting line

One-half the thickness of the shoulder pad

Add 1 in. from the back cutting line at the neckline and taper to the seamline just above the vent.

Back

Jacket hemline

Vent facing

⅝ in.

Lining cutting line

Jacket sleeve

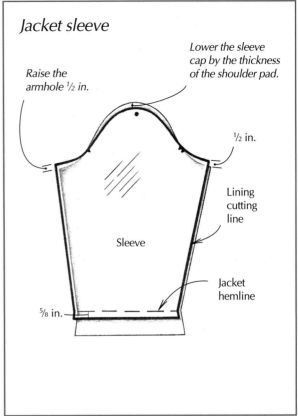

Raise the armhole ½ in.

Lower the sleeve cap by the thickness of the shoulder pad.

½ in.

Lining cutting line

Sleeve

Jacket hemline

⅝ in.

illustration above right). Another way to raise the underarm is by simply taking a ¼-in. seam allowance at the underarm and tapering into the ⅝-in. seamline at the notches when you set in the sleeve. Mark the cutting line to be ⅝ in. longer than the finished sleeve length. If you're making a two-piece sleeve, you will need to make the same lining adjustments as with the one-piece sleeve (see the illustration at right).

Two-piece sleeve

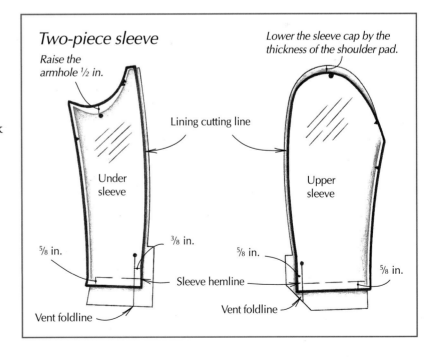

Raise the armhole ½ in.

Lower the sleeve cap by the thickness of the shoulder pad.

Lining cutting line

Under sleeve

Upper sleeve

⅝ in.

3/8 in.

⅝ in.

⅝ in.

Sleeve hemline

Vent foldline

Vent foldline

LINING A JACKET WITH FACINGS THAT CURVE INTO THE ARMHOLE

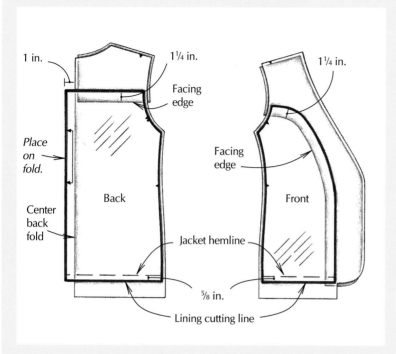

1 in.

1¼ in.

Facing edge

Place on fold.

Center back fold

Back

Facing edge

1¼ in.

Front

Jacket hemline

Lining cutting line

⅝ in.

Unlined jacket patterns often have a wide shoulder facing that reaches into the armhole instead of a back neck facing. The front facings also curve into the armhole. If your fashion fabric isn't too thick or heavily textured, use the same lining principles to create the lining pattern. For both front and back, place the jacket pattern on top of the facing pattern. Mark the lining cutting line 1¼ in. from the facing's edge, then mark the lining

cutting line ⅝ in. below the finished jacket length. Cut the back lining with a center pleat.

You could also change the wide facings to standard facings by changing the shoulder width of the front facing to 3½ in. Draw a new cutting line that blends from the 3½-in. width to the original cutting line approximately one-third of the way down. Create a new curved back neck facing that is 3½ in. wide.

Making a Partial Lining Pattern

A partial lining works well on simple jackets with no pockets or patch pockets because the inside is neat. If the jacket has inside pockets, detailed seams, or other construction details to conceal, use a full lining for the front and a partial lining for the back. Cutting a partial lining follows the same basic principles as cutting a full lining with a few variations. Keep things simple by eliminating the back neck facing and the back pleat if there is one. I often retain the back neck facing on jackets without collars, depending on the fabric and lining combination and how stable or well matched they are, so as not to run the lining to the jacket's outer edge.

Using the back pattern piece, cut the back lining to extend 4 in. below the armhole at the side seams. Lower the front and back shoulder at the armhole by one-half the thickness of the shoulder pad and taper to the original line near the neck (see the illustration at left on the facing page). If the jacket has a center seam, eliminate it from the lining. Place the center back on the fold without adding a back pleat.

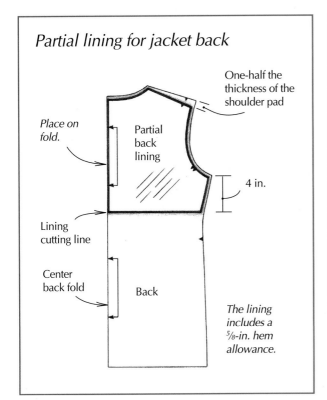

Partial lining for jacket back

One-half the thickness of the shoulder pad

Place on fold.

Partial back lining

4 in.

Lining cutting line

Center back fold

Back

The lining includes a ⅝-in. hem allowance.

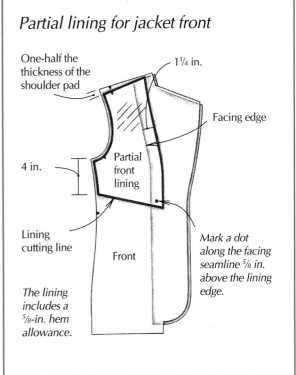

Partial lining for jacket front

One-half the thickness of the shoulder pad

1¼ in.

Facing edge

4 in.

Partial front lining

Lining cutting line

Front

Mark a dot along the facing seamline ⅝ in. above the lining edge.

The lining includes a ⅝-in. hem allowance.

With the jacket front pattern on top of the front facing pattern, line up the outer edges and mark the front lining cutting line 1¼ in. beyond the facing's inner edge. Cut the front lining to extend 4 in. below the armhole at the side seams, then connect the lining to the front facing either straight across or by angling the hem downward (see the illustration above right). Next, mark a dot along the facing seamline ⅝ in. above the lining edge to help you match the hemmed lining to the facing when you attach the lining. Cut the sleeve lining the same as for

a full lining, or eliminate the sleeve lining and bind the armhole.

Constructing and Inserting a Full Lining

After preparing the jacket, the next step is to construct the lining and then insert it. You can insert the lining in one of two ways—by using the modified hand method or by using the machine method, called "bagging the lining."

Lower facing finishing options include (from left to right) overlocking and fusible web; whipstitching by hand; and using a Hong Kong finish and fusible web or slipstitching to hold the facing in place at the hem.

Use a long blind catchstitch about 2 in. in from the jacket front edge to hold the jacket facing to the jacket front.

Preparing the jacket

Before inserting the lining, sew the jacket and sleeve hems, sew in the shoulder pads, and press the jacket perfectly. This is also the best time to machine-sew buttonholes, especially if there are buttonholes on the sleeve vent.

There are several ways to finish the bottom inner edges of the front facings. You can trim the raw edges of the front facings just enough to neaten, then whip-stitch the edges to the hem by hand. You can also overlock the facing edges, then use a small piece of fusible web to secure them to the hem. A third way to finish the lower facing edges is to bind 4 in. near the hem using the lining fabric and a Hong Kong finish, then use fusible web or a slipstitch to hold in place along the jacket hem.

I like to secure the front facings to the jacket fronts because this helps the jacket maintain a smooth appearance on the outside as well as on the inside. Secure the facings between the outward curve of the facing and the hem by pinning the facings about 2 in. from the front edges. Fold back the facings near the pins and sew to the jacket fronts using a long blind catchstitch. A blind catchstitch is the same as a catchstitch except that it is hidden between the hem and

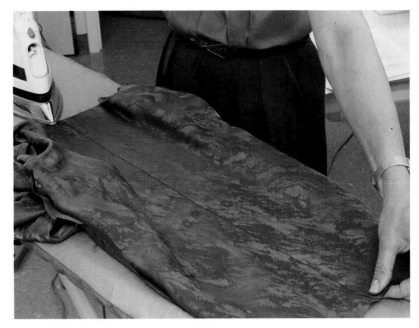

The back pleat is sewn at the top, waist, and lower edge, then pressed to one side into a sharp crease.

the garment. You can spread out the stitches so they are about 1 in. apart.

Sewing the lining

First, sew the center back seam if there is one. Do *not* machine-baste the back pleat because doing so leaves unnecessary holes in the lining. Instead, sew the back pleat along the center back for 1 in. to 2 in. at the top, waist, and lower edge, being sure to lock in the stitch (see the tip on p. 32). Press the center back fold flat to get a sharp crease, then fold to one side along the stitched pleat and press again.

Next, staystitch ½ in. along the back neck curve. The stay-stitching helps to stabilize the

Backstitching can cause puckers on thin lining fabrics. Instead of backstitching, turn the fabric around and sew back over the stitch in the opposite direction, thus locking the stitch. I sew the back pleat starting at the cut edge, then turn the fabric around, and sew all the way back to the cut edge again. Sew the waist pleat starting at the center and sew to either end, turn the fabric around, and sew to the opposite end. Then turn the fabric around and sew back to the center.

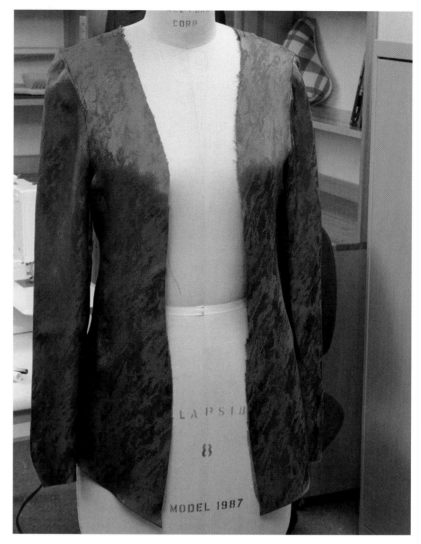

The fully assembled lining is carefully pressed and ready to insert using the modified hand method or the bagged lining technique. If you are using the bagged lining method, leave an opening along one of the lining sleeves.

back neck curve and allows you to clip the seam allowance when you install the lining, making the sewing easier. Sew darts and pleats if any, then connect the remaining lining sections, including setting in the sleeves. Press seams flat, then press open, clipping where necessary. Press waist darts or pleats in the opposite direction of the jacket darts or pleats. Reinforce the underarm seam by stitching again $\frac{1}{8}$ in. inside the first stitching line, starting and stopping near the notches. Trim the seam allowance to $\frac{3}{8}$ in., then press the seam toward the sleeve.

Inserting the lining with the modified hand method

The hand method of inserting a lining is really a modified hand method. In classic tailoring, you sew the lining unit and sleeves into the jacket by hand. In the modified hand version, you sew all the lining sections together by machine, including setting in the sleeves and connecting the lining unit to the facings, then you do the finishing steps by hand.

Hand-sewn finishes are synonymous with fine tailoring and custom-made clothing. The advantage of sewing the finishing steps by hand is that you have better control of the fabric and you can allow for minor sewing imperfections by adjusting the lining. Hand finishing is also an advantage when connecting the lining to velvets and other napped fabrics that tend to slide easily.

Begin inserting the lining by staystitching ½ in. along the lining hem. Press the hem back along the staystitching. The staystitching serves as a guide for pressing back the hem allowance and cuts down on stretching when you press.

Pin the lining unit to the jacket facings. Place the pins perpendicular to the seam with the

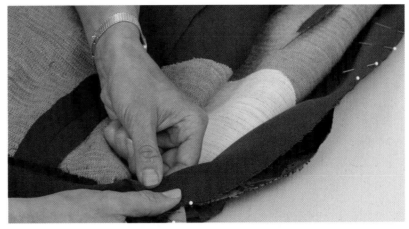

Although the lining fabric may appear to have too much ease when you are pinning it to the front facing, you will be able to align the edges if you pin the pieces flat on a table with the lining placed underneath the front facing.

heads hanging off the edges so you can pull the pins out from either side. When pinning, first match the center back, then the shoulder seams, then the lower front edges. It will be easier to pin the back neck curve if you first clip the lining every ½ in. between the shoulder seams.

Pin the front edges from the bottom up to force the ease to the upper off-grain section of the front facings. If you are using a soft lining fabric, this section may appear to have too much ease but it doesn't. The easiest way to pin this area is by placing the seam flat on a table with the lining underneath the facing. This way the soft lining does not bow away and you will be able to align the edges.

Stitching next to the stay-stitching, sew the back neck section between the shoulder

Using a press cloth to protect the fabric, press the lining into position with the seam allowances toward the lining.

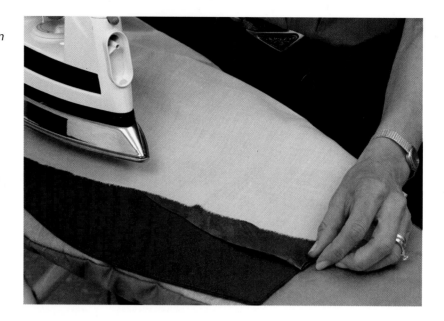

To make a jump hem, pin the lining so that it just covers the hem edge of the jacket and forms a fold of fabric.

Smooth the excess lining toward the hem, then slipstitch the unsewn front edge of the lining to the jacket facing.

seams with the lining on top. Next, placing the facings on top, sew the front edges from the bottom up, leaving 4 in. unstitched near the hem. Stitch 1 in. past the shoulder seams to secure the ends. I find it easier to stitch the back neck section with the lining on top and the front sections with the facings on top, thus sewing this seam in three steps but saving time in the long run. Press the seam flat, then press the seam allowances toward the lining (see the top photo on the facing page). Also press back the ⅝-in. seam allowance that was left unstitched at both lower front lining edges. This lengthwise fold folds over the pressed hemline.

Once the front and back facing sections are sewn, the first step in finishing is to form the jump hem. A jump hem is a horizontal pleat formed at the bottom of the lining hem. This extra length of lining allows for normal differences in the fabric layers and how they move. Fabrics have a different hand, drape, and stability, so any time you sew two different fabrics together, these differences can cause pulling and distortion on the outside garment. The jump hem ensures there is enough ease in the lining for normal body movement when you wear the jacket.

To make the jump hem, pin the folded edge of the lining so that it just covers the hem edge, then slipstitch in place (see the bottom photo on the facing page). Repeat this for both sleeve lining hems. At the front facings, smooth the lining toward the hem, pin, and

At the sleeve hem, fold the raw edge of the lining hem to line up with the raw edge of the jacket hem.

With the jacket sleeve and lining sleeve inside out, repin the edges with right sides facing.

slipstitch the lining to the facings. Press the jump hem to form a soft fold.

After the lining is in place, secure the lining shoulder seams to the shoulder pads and the lining armscye to the jacket armscye by using a pickstitch and sewing in the well of the lining seam. Sew just the lower one-third of the armscye, being sure the stitches do not show on the outside.

Inserting the lining by machine

If you would like to install the lining completely by machine, as is done in ready-to-wear, then this bagged lining technique is for you.

Follow the instructions on p. 31 for preparing the jacket, being sure to hem the jacket and sleeve hems at least 1 in. below the cut edge. As an alternative to hand-sewing the hems, you may use a narrow strip of fusible web to hold the jacket hems in place.

Sew the lining sections together following the directions on pp. 31-32, but leave a long section of one sleeve seam unstitched. If the jacket has a two-piece sleeve, leave one sleeve seam partially open, preferably where there is little or no ease. Keep in mind that the entire jacket must be pulled through this opening. If the jacket is bulky or voluminous,

you can leave most of the seam open, stitching just the top or bottom for about 1 in. Do not staystitch and do not press back the lining hem.

Pin and stitch the lining to the facings following the instructions on pp. 33-34, but instead of leaving the 4 in. of fabric unstitched at the bottom, fold the raw edge of the lining hem to line up with the raw edge of the jacket hem. Stitch the lining to the facings with right sides together, then press the seam flat to set the stitching. Turn the jacket right side out, then press the facing seam toward the lining.

To connect the sleeve and lining hems, position each lining sleeve into each jacket sleeve with wrong sides together (the way you would wear the jacket). Turn back and pin the sleeve lining to the sleeve at the hem near the underarm seam, making sure the sleeves are not twisted (see the top photo on the facing page).

Pull the sleeve through the bottom hem opening to the wrong side. Remove the pin at the underarm seam and stuff the lining sleeve into the jacket sleeve so that you can align the raw edges with right sides together (see the bottom photo on the facing page). Pin and stitch the edges together using a ⅝-in. seam allowance (see the top photo on p. 38).

Stitch the sleeve and lining together using a ⅝-in. seam allowance.

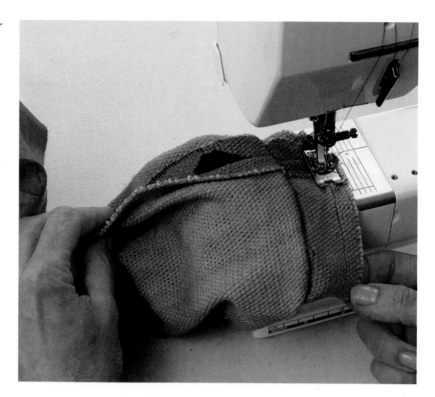

Sew the jacket and lining hem together, getting as close as possible to the front facings.

After pulling the jacket right side out through the sleeve, close the sleeve seam with an edgestitch.

If the jacket sleeve has a vent, start sewing the lining near the vent and end as close as possible to the other side of the opening. There will be a small gap as there is at the lower front hem near the facings. Pull the sleeve through to the right side. Repeat for the second sleeve.

Next, connect the jacket and lining hems. If the jacket has a center back or side back vents, connect the vertical vent seams with right sides facing (see Chapter 10 on sewing vents). Pin the jacket hem to the lining hem with right sides together.

Sew the jacket and lining hems together, getting as close as possible to the front facings (see the bottom photo on the facing page).

Press the seam flat to set the stitching and pull the jacket right side out through the sleeve opening. Press the extra lining or jump hem toward the bottom to form a crease. Close the sleeve lining seam by pinning and sewing the folded edges together using an edgestitch (see the photo above).

Before pinning the entire hem with right sides together, pin each front lining edge in place to prevent shifting. Start with the right side of the lining facing up (the wrong side of the lining facing the wrong side of the jacket). At each front edge next to the front facings, reach between the lining and jacket to pin the hem edges together with right sides facing. Pin for a distance of about 6 in., then turn the entire hem with right sides together and pin the remaining hem to the lining.

ADDING DECORATIVE PIPING

Why not make the inside of a jacket or coat as interesting as the outside, or close to it. Once you start using different linings instead of one that simply matches the outside color, you'll find it difficult to settle for the perfect match. Prints, jacquards, contrasting colors, and quilted fabrics are interesting alternatives to the perfect match that enliven the inside of the jacket.

Another easy way to add a decorative finishing touch to the inside of your jacket or coat is to use bias piping between the lining and the facings. You can purchase piping if you like the selection or you can sew your own. If you sew your own, use blouse or lining fabric in either a matching or contrasting color to the lining. Striped fabrics cut on the bias create an interesting diagonally striped edge. Consider using alternatives to bias piping such as purchased braided trim or soutache. I also like to use

rickrack. When the rickrack is centered on the seam, only half will show to form a triangular picot edge.

To add piping, cut 1¾-in.-wide bias strips of fabric a few inches longer than the length of the facing seam. Fold the fabric around a ⅛-in. cording or yarn, then machine-baste close to the cording with a piping or zipper foot (**1**). Pin the piping to the right side of the front facing, starting at the front hem and matching the raw edges (**2**). Baste in place.

Pin the lining to the facings with right sides together, being sure to fold the raw edge of the lining hem to line up with the raw edge of the jacket hem (**3**). Fold the ends of the piping over the lining hem, trim the piping the same length as the lining, and stitch the lining in place using a zipper foot. To reduce bulk when you fold the piping over the hem, you can also trim the inside cording so that it ends at the lining fold.

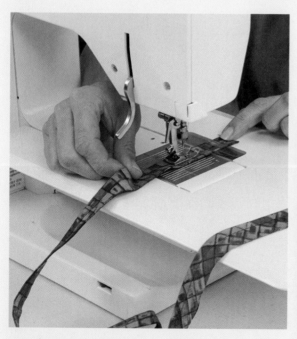

1 *When assembling piping, baste bias-cut binding close to the cording using a piping or zipper foot. If using piping cut on the crossgrain, baste with a standard foot and a ³⁄₈-in. seam allowance.*

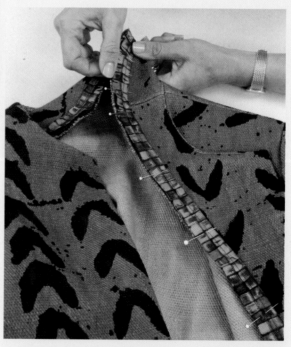

2 *Pin the piping to the right side of the front facing, starting at the front hem and working your way around, and baste in place.*

Stitch with the facing side up, sewing over the previous stitches. Press the seam flat to set the stitching. Turn the jacket right side out and press the seam allowance toward the lining. You may also remove the entire cording, which is used as a way to keep the width of the bias binding consistent, after the piping is stitched in place. Doing this results in a flatter piping.

An alternative to corded bias piping is to cut or tear crosswise strips of fabric, depending on the elasticity of the lining fabric you are using and the shape of the facing's curve. The advantage is that tearing the binding is faster, easier, and more accurate. You also eliminate the need for cording because the crosswise fabric is more stable and stays a consistent width. You can sew all steps using the standard presser foot.

Tear crosswise strips $1\frac{3}{4}$ in. wide. Fold in half lengthwise with wrong sides facing, then machine-baste using a $\frac{3}{8}$-in. seam allowance. Pin in place to the right side of the facing edge, aligning the raw edges. Clip the piping to the machine-baste stitch where it follows the facing curves at $\frac{1}{2}$-in. intervals, then machine-baste to the facings over the previous baste.

Whether using bias-cut or crosswise-cut strips, pin the lining to the facings with right sides together, being sure to fold the raw edge of the lining hem to line up with the raw edge of the jacket hem (**4**). If using crosswise-cut strips, trim the length of the piping $\frac{1}{2}$ in. below the lining hem fold, then tuck the piping ends into the piping fold with wrong sides together so the lower edge of the piping lines up with the lower fold of the lining (**5**). You may have to unstitch a few basting stitches. Stitch the lining in place using a regular presser foot and a $\frac{5}{8}$-in. seam allowance.

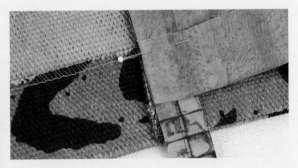

4 Fold up the raw edge of the lining to meet the raw edge of the jacket hem, then pin in place.

3 Pin the lining to the basted piping and facing, aligning all raw edges.

5 Finish the ends on crosswise-cut piping by tucking the ends of the piping into itself and pressing for a clean finish.

LINING SIMPLE OR REVERSIBLE JACKETS WITH THE BAGGED LINING TECHNIQUE

To line a simple jacket to the edge or to sew a reversible jacket with the bagged lining method, cut the lining the same as the jacket, both having a $\frac{5}{8}$-in. hem allowance. Sew the jacket, then the lining. If sewing a jacket to be lined to the edge, leave an opening in one of the lining sleeve seams that is long enough to pull the jacket through.

Attach the lining to the jacket at the front edges and neck seam, then reach between the layers and sew the sleeve hems together.

If sewing a reversible jacket, sew the hems together with right sides facing, leaving an opening along the back hemline just past one of the side seams so you can pull the jacket right side out.

For a jacket lined to the edge, close the entire hem and pull the jacket right side out through the sleeve opening. To finish, edgestitch the sleeve opening or slipstitch the hem opening. Another finishing option is to edgestitch the entire front opening and hem or to use fusible web at the hem opening.

Constructing and Inserting a Partial Lining

A partial lining keeps a jacket lightweight and cool. You can customize the lining by placing it where it will do the most good, keeping in mind how you will wear the jacket and whether there are inside construction details to cover. For example, I like to wear simple, short, boxy jackets, buttoned and without a blouse. I also like to push up the sleeves. The best lining solution for this is to use a partial front and back lining and to eliminate the sleeve lining. Tailored jackets with inside details such as

interfacing and welt pockets need a full front lining, but a partial lining can be used for the back and a full lining can be used for the sleeves. You can line jackets that have easy shapes and little inside tailoring using a partial front and partial back lining. Lining the sleeves is optional. Another way to partially line a jacket is to completely line the body and not line the sleeves.

On all these partial lining variations, the back lining section covers the shoulder area and stops about 4 in. below the armhole. The lower edge hangs free instead of being connected to the jacket. Normally, the back neck facing is eliminated so the back lining connects directly to the neckseam. This is a lightweight and easy way to finish the shoulder area. But there is also the option of adding the back neck facing and connecting the partial lining to the facing as I've done on a sample garment. In this case, the back neck facing balances the weight and thickness of the front facing. The lining fabric is a delicate silk and the facing covers the area of the jacket most likely to wear.

Hem interfacings should be cut $\frac{1}{4}$ in. less than the finished hem so the interfacings are not visible. Any exposed seams and hems can be covered with a bias-bound finish, such as a Hong

USING A HONG KONG FINISH

A Hong Kong finish is used to cover exposed seams and hems. Begin by cutting 1½-in.-wide bias binding from the lining fabric. Stitch to the seam allowance with right sides together, ¼ in. from the edge. Wrap the bias around the raw seam edges and press. Stitch from the right side in the well of the seam. Trim the unfinished bias edge if necessary.

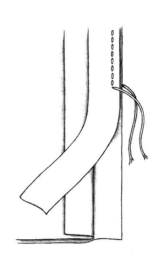

Stitch bias fabric to the seam with right sides facing using a ¼-in. seam allowance.

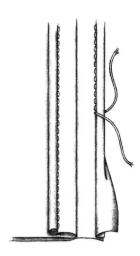

Wrap the bias around the seam allowance and stitch in the well of the seam to finish.

Kong finish (see the sidebar above), with purchased bias tape, or by overlocking the seams.

Sewing the partial lining

Sew the partial front and partial back lining sections at the side seams. Press back the hem ¼ in., then press again ⅜ in. and stitch close to the inner fold. If you are connecting a partial back lining to a full front lining, hem the back lining before sewing the side seams. Sew the shoulder seams and attach the sleeves. (If there is no back facing, sew the shoulder seams and attach the sleeves to the lining after connecting the front lining to

the front facings. In this case, connect the facings and lining as a unit to the jacket's outer edge.)

Inserting the partial lining

Before connecting the partial front lining to the jacket, bind the inner edge of the front facings from the bottom to 1½ in. above where the lining meets the facings. Also bind all seams and hems that will remain exposed after the lining is in place. Hem the jacket and sleeves using a blind catchstitch. If you are using a full front lining, you don't have to bind or edge finish the front facings, front hem, and other seams

The partial lining is ready to be inserted into the jacket after the side and shoulder seams are sewn and the sleeves are attached.

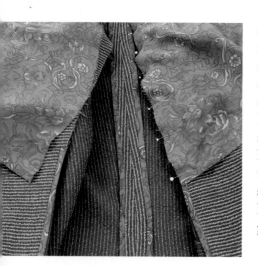

Finish the facings and seam allowances that will remain exposed, then pin the partial lining to the front facing edge.

covered by the front lining. Connect the lining unit to the facing edge. Be sure to fold up the lining hem to line up with the jacket hem when sewing the full front lining to the front facing. Press the seam allowance flat, then press toward the lining.

Connect the sleeve hems using the bagged lining technique (see pp. 37-39). Reach between the layers and sew the hems with right sides together. If you eliminate the sleeve lining, machine-baste the lining armscye to the jacket armscye with wrong sides facing. Bind the edges together using a Hong Kong finish.

If you are using a full front lining, machine-sew the lining hem to the jacket hem by reaching between the layers and sewing with right sides together. At the side seams, you can either turn the lining under and slipstitch it to the front seam allowance or turn it under ¼ in. and edgestitch it to the back seam allowance. If you are using a partial front lining, secure the lining hem to the jacket seam allowances at each side seam by hand or machine. You can tack the lining directly to the jacket seam allowances or you can use French tacks or quick tacks (see pp. 53-54).

Adding Underarm Shields

If you often wear jackets over sleeveless tops or shells, consider adding underarm shields to the jacket lining to protect the underarm area from the damage caused by perspiration or chemicals. Perspiration and chemicals in deodorant deteriorate silk, cotton, and rayon.

An easy shape to use for the shields is an oval with an inward curve at the center. To construct the shields, cut or tear four rectangles approximately 5½ in. wide by 8 in. long from the lining fabric. Form the inward curve at the center by folding the 8-in. length in half with right sides together, then stitching or overlocking a horizontal dart that tapers at both ends. Sewing the dart ¾ in. wide at the center works for most armholes. Cut away the two outer corners with a curved line to form half an oval. Use the first oval to trim the other ovals so they are all the same.

Another way to shape the dart is by copying the lower armhole curve. Place the folded fabric oval under the sleeve or jacket pattern at the armhole and copy the curve, raising the center ½ in.

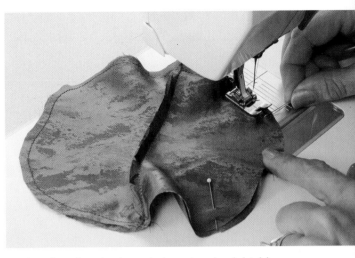

Use the first oval as a guide to trim the other ovals for underarm shields.

With right sides together, stitch each pair of shields using a ⅛-in. to ¼-in. seam allowance and leaving a 1-in. opening along a straight part of the seam.

Stitch the dart on all four sections and trim the seam allowance to ¼ in. Clip the curve and press open or to one side. Stitch each pair of shields with right sides facing with a ⅛-in. to ¼-in. seam allowance, leaving a 1-in. opening. Turn right side out, press the edges, and close the opening using a slipstitch, an edgestitch, or a piece of fusible web.

After the lining has been inserted into the jacket, sew each shield to the lining underarm using a long slipstitch so the shields are easily removed when you want to clean or replace them.

When sewn to the lining with a long slipstitch, underarm shields are easily removed to replace or clean.

LINING A BASEBALL OR BLOUSON JACKET

The baseball jacket is an American classic. The shape has a relaxed fit that is comfortable and easy to wear. Although baseball or blouson jackets are usually considered sporty, they also look wonderful in luxurious or dressy fabrics or when sewn reversibly using two lightweight fabrics.

To fully line a blouson jacket by machine, assemble the jacket body above the ribbing or casing, including setting in the sleeves, attaching the ribbing to the sleeves only, and sewing the collar in place.

If your pattern does not include a lining, make your own by applying the basic guidelines on pp. 22-27. Since blouson styles are loose fitting, you don't have to add a back pleat or a jump hem; just allow for the facings. There are several possible style variations for which the sewing sequence is basically the same. When the jacket has a front zipper, you may eliminate the facings and cut the lining using the jacket pattern. You can also make the jacket reversible, as the one shown here.

Sew the front facings to the back neck facing. Assemble the lining pieces, then connect to the facing unit. If the jacket doesn't have a back neck facing, sew the front facing to the front lining before sewing the lining at the shoulder seams. Leave an opening along one of the lining sleeves to be able to turn the jacket right side out if the jacket you are sewing has a button closure. On jackets with a zipper closure, you can use the front edge to turn the jacket right side out when you bag the lining (1). Press seams open and facing seams toward the lining.

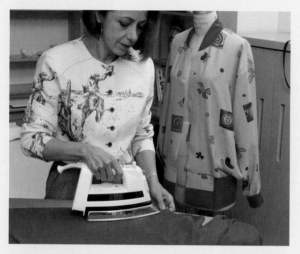

1 The jacket is sewn to one edge of the lower band. The sleeve linings are fully sewn, as this jacket will be turned right side out through the front edge.

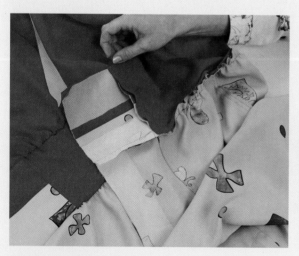

2 With the jacket attached to one edge of the ribbing, pin and sew the lining to the other edge with right sides together.

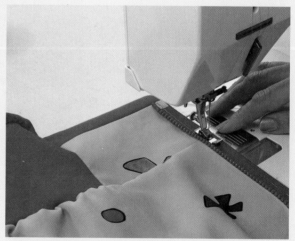

3 Unfold the pressed front edges and baste the separating zipper to the jacket seam allowance, aligning the zipper teeth next to the fold.

Next, pin and stitch the lower front band to each end of the ribbing with right sides together. With the band open, connect the jacket to one side of the band with right sides together, then connect the lining unit to the other side, also with right sides together (2). If the jacket has a separating zipper, press back the front edges to mark the center front but unfold to baste the zipper in place (3). Press back the front edge on the front facings or lining.

Pin and stitch the lining to the jacket at the neck seam with right sides together if there is a separating zipper. If the jacket has a button closure, also pin and stitch the front edges with right sides together. Grade and clip seams, then turn the jacket right side out

through the sleeve opening or the zipper opening (4). Reach between the layers through the opening to pin and stitch the ribbing edges wrong sides together (5). Sew as close to the front edges as possible.

Connect the sleeve lining to the ribbing. Reach through the opening to pin the lining hem to the ribbing with right sides together. Be careful not to twist the sleeves. The sleeve and sleeve lining should be right sides together with the ribbed cuff in between (6). Repeat for the second sleeve.

Pin the front edges, aligning the front and facing edges to finish the zipper application by topstitching through all the layers. On jackets with a button closure, edgestitch the sleeve opening.

5 Reach through the zipper or sleeve opening to pin and stitch the edges of the ribbing together.

4 After grading and clipping seams, turn the jacket right side out through the zipper opening or through the sleeve opening if the jacket has buttons.

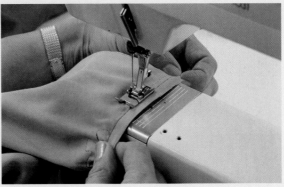

6 Sew the sleeve and sleeve lining with right sides together and the ribbing in between, making sure the lining isn't twisted.

3 | *Coat Linings*

Coat linings should be durable, beautiful, and in some cases warm. Durability is important because coat linings are subjected to more wear than those in other garments. Coat linings should also be smooth so they don't cling to the variety of fabrics you wear under them. Good choices for coat linings include polyester and microfiber fabrics, which are very durable and come in a variety of weights; satin, twill, faille, and taffeta; and heavier rayon, polyester, and silk jacquard fabrics.

Many lining fabrics that are appropriate for jackets can also be used for coats, but I prefer to use a heavier lining fabric because the fashion fabric is also heavier. If you live in a cold climate or select a fashion fabric that is lightweight, you may want to use a lining that is intended for outerwear to add warmth. One such outerwear lining fabric that is warm yet luxurious has a satin face and a flannel backing. You might also want to consider a quilted lining if it isn't too stiff. The color range of these specialty linings is limited, so when a complementary color is not available, you can interline a standard lining fabric with an insulating layer of fabric such as flannel or Thinsulate.

In this chapter, I'll show you how to make a lining pattern and how to construct and insert a standard coat lining. I'll also discuss how to replace an old coat lining and how to make a coat more versatile by sewing a zip-out lining.

Making a Coat Lining Pattern

Most coat patterns provide a lining pattern but if not, you can easily create one. To create a lining pattern from a coat pattern, position the front facing pattern under the front pattern, making sure the notches match. The inner edge of the front facing is the reference for cutting the lining. The lining will need ⅝ in. to reach the sewing line along the facing and another ⅝ in. as a seam allowance.

Using a sewing gauge, draw the lining cutting line 1¼ in. from the inner facing edge. Mark "lining cutting line" on the front pattern, then mark the cutting length of the lining to be the length of the finished coat plus ⅝ in. Lower the front and back shoulder at the armhole by one-half the thickness of the shoulder pad and taper to the original line near the neck (see the illustrations below). Place the back neck facing pattern under the back coat pattern, aligning the outer edges. Mark the lining cutting line 1¼ in. from the

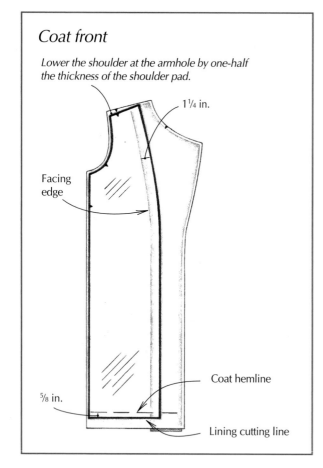

Coat front

Lower the shoulder at the armhole by one-half the thickness of the shoulder pad.

1¼ in.

Facing edge

Coat hemline

⅝ in.

Lining cutting line

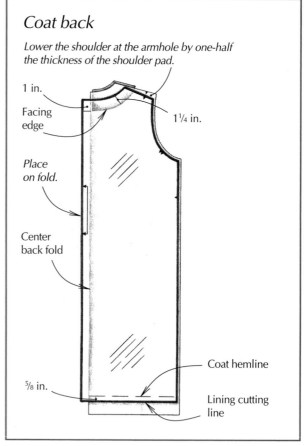

Coat back

Lower the shoulder at the armhole by one-half the thickness of the shoulder pad.

1 in.

Facing edge

1¼ in.

Place on fold.

Center back fold

Coat hemline

⅝ in.

Lining cutting line

facing's inner edge and mark the cutting length ⅝ in. below the coat's finished length. When you cut the lining, add a center back pleat by placing the center back 1 in. from the fabric fold.

To create a one- or two-piece sleeve lining, follow the directions on pp. 26-27. Your coat, however, may have raglan sleeves, which are common on roomy coats and jackets and are sometimes found on dresses. The raglan sleeve extends past the shoulder and ends at the coat neckline, so the lining pattern adjustment must allow for the facings on the sleeves as well as on the front and back. The best way to create the lining pattern from the coat pattern is to pin the front sleeve to the coat front and the back sleeve to the coat back, aligning the sewing lines (see the illustration below). Overlapping the pattern with a 1¼-in. space between the cutting lines is the same as pinning the sewing lines together. Start pinning at the neckline and continue to about halfway to the underarm, where the sleeve and coat patterns begin to overlap.

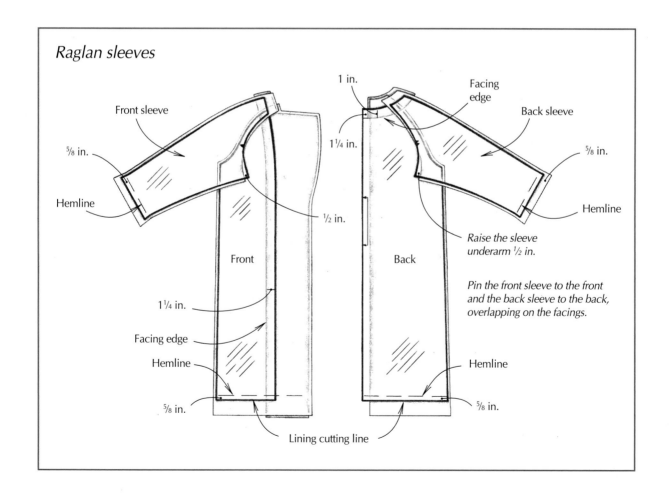

Raglan sleeves

Front sleeve

1 in.

Facing edge

Back sleeve

⅝ in.

1¼ in.

⅝ in.

Hemline

½ in.

Hemline

Front

Raise the sleeve underarm ½ in.

Back

Pin the front sleeve to the front and the back sleeve to the back, overlapping on the facings.

1¼ in.

Facing edge

Hemline

Hemline

⅝ in.

⅝ in.

Lining cutting line

Place the front facing beneath the front and sleeve pattern and the back facing beneath the back and sleeve pattern, aligning the outer edges. Mark the lining cutting line 1¼ in. from the facing's inner edge on the front, front sleeve, back, and back sleeve, then mark the lining cutting length at the front, back, and sleeve hems to be ⅝ in. below the finished garment hemline.

Raise the sleeve armhole at the underarm by ½ in., or make this adjustment during the sewing by using a ¼-in. seam at the underarm that blends into the ⅝-in. seam at the notches. Add a center back pleat when you cut the back by placing the pattern 1 in. from the fabric fold.

The coat may have a shaped back seam. All of the back variations that apply to jackets also apply to coats (see pp. 22-26). If the coat has a center vent, the back lining must have a center seam. See Chapter 10 for directions on adjusting the lining pattern and sewing the vent area.

Constructing and Inserting a Coat Lining

Follow the pattern instructions to assemble the coat. The next step is to sew, then insert the lining. The lining can be inserted by using one of the methods used for jackets—the modified hand method or the bagged lining technique—or by using a third option: a free-hanging hem.

Preparing the coat

Before inserting the lining, begin preparing the coat by sewing in the shoulder pads. Next, machine-sew the buttonholes, including those on the sleeve vents. Sew the coat hem by hand using a blind catchstitch or by machine using a blind-hemming stitch. If you plan to bag the lining (see pp. 37-39), hem the coat and sleeve 1 in. below the hem edge. Lastly, finish the lower facing edges by hand using a whipstitch, by machine using an overlock stitch, or by binding the lower section with a Hong Kong finish. Press the coat.

Sewing the lining

To assemble the lining, begin by sewing the center back seam if there is one. Rather than machine-basting the entire back pleat, sew the pleat along the center back for 1 in. to 2 in. at the top, waist, and lower edge, being sure to lock in the stitch. Press the center back fold flat into a sharp crease, then fold to one side along the stitched pleat and press again.

Next, staystitch ½ in. along the back neckline curve and sew any darts and pleats. After sewing

HEMMING METHOD FOR HEAVY FABRICS

Coat hems can get heavy, making it difficult to hem invisibly. When hemming a heavy fabric, add a layer of fusible or sew-in interfacing to the hem to support the hem and cushion the stitches from the outside layer. You can apply light- to medium-weight bias-cut fusible interfacing to the hem edge or use interfacing with a crosswise stretch. I like to use fusible weft insertion or warp insertion interfacings because they support the fabric without making it stiff.

To use this method, cut the interfacing 1½ in. wider than the hem allowance and fuse the interfacing so its lower edge is ½ in. below the marked hemline, making sure not to fuse over the seam allowances. Cut the interfacing so that it meets the stitch line under the seam allowances. The interfacing will show above the turned-up hem and keep the hem edge from leaving an impression on the outside. When you sew an unlined garment using this technique, cut the interfacing about ¼ in. wider than the hem allowance.

Extra heavy or wide hems also benefit from being stitched twice. To do this, turn the hem allowance up and baste just below the center of the hem. Fold the hem back just above the basting and sew in place using a blind catchstitch, spacing the stitches about ½ in. apart. Finally, secure the hem a second time close to the upper edge using a blind catchstitch.

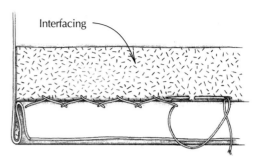

Use a blind catchstitch to stitch the hem about halfway.

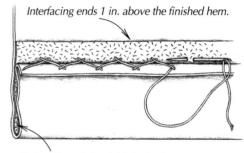

½ in. of interfacing folds in the hem.

Stitch the hem again just below the upper edge of the fabric.

the lining body together, press seams flat, then open, clipping where necessary. Waist darts or pleats should be pressed in the opposite direction of the coat darts or pleats. Once the sleeves are sewn in, reinforce the armhole by stitching in the seam allowance ⅛ in. away from the first stitch, then trim the seam allowance to ⅜ in. Press the seam toward the sleeve.

Inserting the free-hanging lining

Most ready-to-wear coats have a free-hanging lining hem, which is fast and easy to do. For this technique, you can use either French tacks or quick tacks to fasten the lining hem to the coat hem while allowing for some movement between the two hems. To finish a free-hanging

The classic French tack is easy to sew but takes a little time.

Quick tacks are just that, with one end sewn into the lining hem and the other sewn into the coat hem.

lining, pin and sew the lining unit to the coat facings, leaving 4 in. unstitched at each front edge near the hem. Then sew the sleeve lining hem to the sleeve hem by hand using a slipstitch or by machine using the bagged lining method (see pp. 37-39).

If you choose to use French tacks, begin by hemming the coat lining to be 1 in. shorter than the coat using a topstitch, a machine blind-hemming stitch, or a slipstitch. Finish sewing the front edge of the hemmed lining to the front facings, then connect the coat hem to the lining hem at the side seams using French tacks.

To do this, take a stitch at each side seam near the top of the hem edge, hiding the knot under the hem, then stitch through the lining hem, leaving a 1-in. to 2-in. slack between stitches. Repeat this stitch, alternating between the coat hem and the lining hem to form the foundation stitches, then work closely spaced blanket stitches over the foundation stitches. Use a strand of the same all-purpose thread used to sew the garment or sew using a single strand of thick thread such as buttonhole twist because it is easier to sew without getting tangled.

The other option is to use quick tacks, which is my name for an easy way to secure the lining hem to the coat hem that comes

from ready-to-wear. This method uses narrow ribbon, soutache, or narrow and flat braid instead of the hand-stitching. To use quick tacks, start by pressing but not stitching the lining hem. Cut two 4-in. lengths of ribbon and insert one end of each piece of ribbon under the pressed-back lining hem at each side seam, then machine-stitch the entire lining hem to catch the ribbon. Finish sewing the front edge of the hemmed lining to the front facings, and connect the loose ends of ribbon to the coat hem, tucking under or cutting away as much of the ribbon as necessary to form 2-in. tacks. Sew the ribbon in place using a hand-stitch or machine-stitch to the hem allowance.

Replacing an Old Coat Lining

Replacing a lining is easy because you can use the old lining to determine how much lining fabric to buy and also use it as the pattern to cut the new one.

Removing the old lining

Before removing the old lining, mark matchpoints that are 4 in. above the bottom hem at the front facing and extend onto the lining. Also mark the lining sleeve where the shoulder seam meets the sleeve cap. To allow you to identify the sleeve front

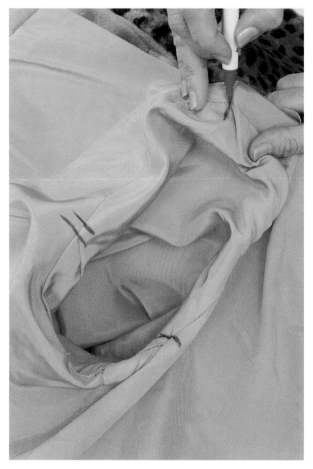 

Before removing the old lining, indicate matchpoints with a fabric marker where the lining sleeve meets the body, making two marks on the back sleeve so you can tell it apart from the front later. Also place a mark where the shoulder meets the sleeve cap.

When removing the old lining from the facing, use a seam ripper so you don't damage the coat fabric.

and back, place a single matchpoint along the front armscye 4 in. from the underarm seam and double matchpoints the same distance away along the back armscye. If the lining has a two-piece sleeve, place matchpoints where the sleeve seams meet the body and use two marks that are close together for the back sleeve seam.

Remove only half of the lining at first so you can use the remaining section as a reference. Use the side of the lining that is in better condition as your pattern.

Remove half of the lining from the facing using a seam ripper. The easiest way to separate the rest of the lining is by cutting

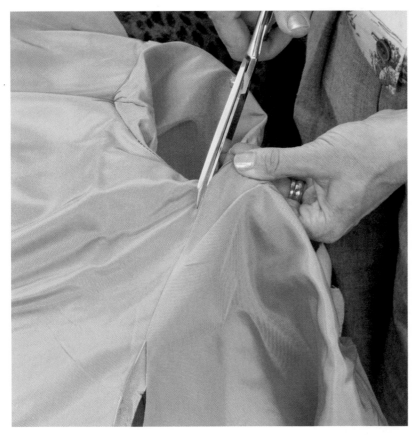

along the stitching lines. I leave in the hem stitching, then add that allowance when cutting the new lining. At the center back, cut along the seam or along the center fold. If the lining has a back vent, carefully remove the stitches connecting the lining to the coat. Finally, press all of the lining sections.

Once the lining is removed, you can use it as a guide for buying fabric for the new one. You will need a fabric amount that is once or twice the length of the old lining body and sleeves plus ⅛ yd. for each length for hems and fabric straightening. If the body of the lining including seam allowances is narrower than the lining fabric, you will need one length; if the body is wider, you'll need twice the length. The same applies to the sleeves, which should be measured from the highest point of the sleeve cap to the hem.

Once you have removed the lining, cut apart the pieces at the seamlines since the lining will only be used as a pattern.

Locating the grain

To locate the lengthwise grain on the old lining to use as a reference when cutting the new one, pull on a lengthwise thread but don't pull it out completely. If pulling the thread gathers the fabric or shifts the thread, then you've found the lengthwise grain. Another way to find the lengthwise grain is by pulling the

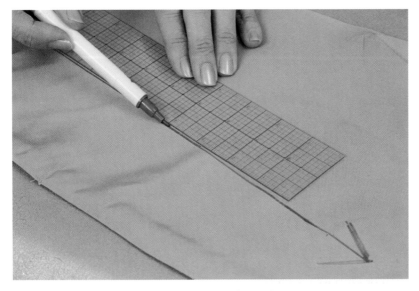

Mark the grainline on each piece of the old coat lining.

top and bottom of each lining section taut. The direction that does not stretch is the lengthwise grain. Once you've found the lengthwise grain, mark the grainline using a ruler and a contrasting marker.

Cutting the new lining

Cut the new lining, adding a ⅝-in. seam allowance and the hem allowance from the original lining. If the style and the fabric width allow, cut the center back on the fold to save time. Be sure to add a center back pleat to cut down on strain across the back even if the original lining doesn't include one. If the coat has a back vent, cut both sides of the back with the extension, then use the original lining as a pattern for marking the sewing and cutting lines for the left side on both back sections. Cut away the left extension after the lining is assembled. (For more on vents, see Chapter 10.)

Sewing the lining

Sew the lining together following the directions on pp. 52-53. If the lining you are replacing has a back vent, see pp. 138-140 on how to sew the vent area.

Adding a Zip-Out Lining

Another way to line a coat is to sew in a permanent lining and a removable one. You normally find zip-out linings in all-weather coats or raincoats, but you can add one to any coat or outerwear jacket that has enough ease to accommodate the extra layer. It's important to select a style that has enough ease to fit over the bulkiest garment you plan to wear under the coat.

In both men's and women's all-weather coats, there are many variations on how the removable lining is connected to the coat. My favorite method sets the edge of the zip-out lining slightly underneath the front facings. By doing it this way, you don't see the binding or the teeth. For this method, you will need a separating zipper that is 80 in. or longer.

Selecting the pattern

Select a coat pattern with raglan, dolman, or dropped-shoulder sleeves and a generous fit. Close-fitting styles and those with narrow set-in sleeves are not appropriate for zip-out linings.

Selecting fabrics

When choosing fabrics, use a standard lining fabric such as a twill or satin weave for the

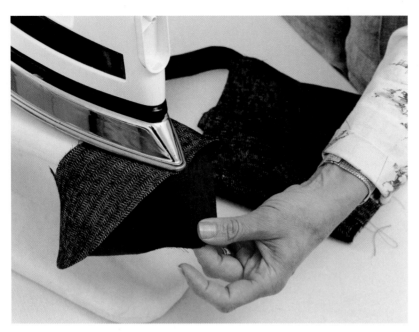

When making a faced back neck facing for a zip-out lining, press the seam allowance toward the uninterfaced facing. Understitch the seam allowance to the uninterfaced facing, then press the facings with wrong sides together.

permanent lining. For the zip-out lining, select a warm fabric such as flannel, fake fur, polyfleece, or quilted fabric. You can also interline or quilt a standard lining fabric using polyester fleece, Thinsulate, or another insulating material. You may use the insulating fabric in the sleeves if the fabric isn't too bulky, but most ready-to-wear coats just have an insulated body while the sleeves have a standard single layer of lining.

Adjusting the coat pattern for a zip-out lining

If the pattern does not include a back neck facing, add one following the directions on pp. 22. You should also increase the coat's shoulder and side-seam allowances to 1 in. to allow for adjustments depending on the

thickness of the lining you select. Since you must use a coat pattern with ample ease, you may omit the center back pleat on both the permanent and zip-out linings. Add ¾ in. to the front facing's inner edge and the permanent lining's outer edge along the front and back facing seams.

Preparing the coat and the permanent lining

Assemble the coat body, leaving the shoulder seams and side seams pinned or basted so you can check the fit. Do not attach the facings yet. Then assemble the permanent lining and press the seams open. If you plan to bag the lining, remember to leave an opening at one of the sleeve seams. Staystitch the back neck curve ¼ in. from the edge.

Preparing the facing unit

Once the pattern has been adjusted, cut two back neck facings, then interface one back neck facing and both front facings to the edge using fusible interfacing. Sewing a faced back neck facing makes it possible to completely hide the separating zipper along the neck curve. To do this, sew the longer curve of the two back neck facings with right sides together, then trim or grade the seam allowance. Press and understitch the seam allowance to the uninterfaced facing, then press the facing with wrong sides together. Using a

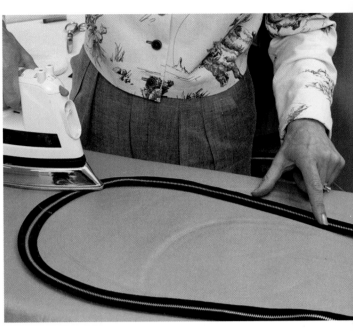

Mark the uninterfaced side of the back neck facing 1⅜ in. from the understitched edge using a fabric marker and a seam gauge, then trim away the excess.

Use plenty of steam to shape the zipper, curving away from the center point. Make the side of the zipper with the zipper pull the outside of the curve.

sewing gauge and a fabric marker, mark the uninterfaced facing 1⅜ in. from the understitched edge and trim away the excess along this line.

Sew the front and back facings together at the shoulder seams, opening the trimmed facing. After pressing the shoulder seams open, trim the seam allowances to ¼ in. to reduce bulk. Press back 1⅜ in. along the inside facing edges to line up with the back facing seam. The crease just formed creates a flange that hides the zipper teeth and will be a guide for pinning the zipper. If necessary for the seam allowance to lie flat, clip the curved edges of the

front facings at ½-in. intervals, being sure to clip no more than ¼ in. deep.

To prepare the zipper for pinning to the facing unit, fold the zipper in half and mark the center using tailor's chalk or another fabric marker. Using a steam iron, curve the zipper near the center mark, making the side with the zipper pull the outside of the curve. By doing this, it will be easier to pin the zipper to the curve of the back neck facing.

Using pins or double-sided basting tape, attach the inner curve of the zipper under the edge of the facing unit, easing the zipper edge at the back neck facing. Start pinning at the

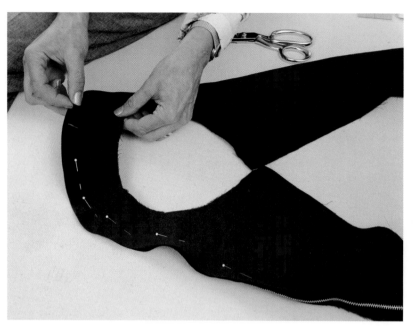

Use the folded facing edge as the reference for positioning the zipper. With right side facing up, place the closed zipper under the facing unit, positioning the zipper teeth ⅜ in. from the folded edge. Starting at the center back, pin the zipper tape as far as possible from the folded edge and closest to the neckline.

center back, positioning the zipper's teeth so they are ⅜ in. from the facing edge. To be sure there is enough ease in the zipper to follow the neck curve, I find it is best to pin from the facing side with the zipper closed, keeping the amount of zipper tape extending beyond the folded facing edge consistent. On a sample garment that I sewed, the width of the zipper tape to either side of the teeth was ⅜ in., so lining up the outer edge of the closed zipper placed the zipper teeth ⅜ in. away from the facing edge or fold.

Topstitch between ⅝ in. and ¾ in. from the facing fold using a zipper foot, starting at the bottom edge of the left front facing and ending at the bottom edge of the right front facing.

Backstitch at both the beginning and the end of the zipper tape to reinforce these stress areas. The line you follow when stitching depends on the sewing machine you are using. On my sample garment, I followed a ¾-in. seam allowance with the needle positioned to the right of center. Doing this resulted in an ¹¹⁄₁₆-in. seam allowance.

Attaching the permanent lining to the facing unit

To attach the permanent lining to the facing unit, begin by separating the zipper so it will be more flexible. Pin the lining to the seam allowance of the facing unit with right sides together, lining up the raw edges and clipping the lining to the staystitching at the back neck curve. Using a zipper foot and a ⅜-in. seam allowance, stitch the lining and facing together, leaving 4 in. unstitched at both hems. Press the seam flat.

Preparing the zip-out lining

After the permanent lining is sewn to the coat facings, cut the zip-out lining using the original lining pattern with the following changes. If the lining fabric is bulky, it is best to bind the outer edges of the zip-out lining. To do this, remove ⅜ in. along the outer edge at the front and back of the neck. If the fabric isn't too bulky, however, use the original lining pattern, then overlock the outside edge and turn under a ³⁄₈-in. seam allowance instead. Naturally, this is faster and easier to do.

Cut the back lining on the fold, eliminating the center back seam and center back pleat. I also like to eliminate the side seams whenever possible because it simplifies the sewing. To be able to do this, the style must have straight side seams and the lining fabric must be wide enough to accommodate the entire lining width. If you're going to eliminate the side seams, pin the pattern pieces together along the side seams using a ³⁄₄-in. seam allowance, then cut the lining fronts and back as one piece.

Cut the lining to a finished length that is 5 in. to 8 in. shorter than the finished coat plus a 1-in. or 2-in. hem allowance. If you are going to bind the hem, you don't need any hem allowance. Because the hem is the only lining edge that is exposed when the lining is in place, I like to bind it to make it look attractive. You can also use binding at the hem when the lining fabric does not topstitch nicely, such as when using fake fur. Finally, cut the sleeves the same length as the finished coat sleeves. This length includes a 1-in. hem allowance.

Sewing the zip-out lining

To assemble the zip-out lining, pin and sew the lining pieces together using a ³⁄₄-in. seam allowance except when sewing in the sleeves. Using a ³⁄₄-in. seam allowance makes the zip-out lining slightly smaller than the coat and permanent lining so it will fit smoothly underneath. You can overlock any seam or edge that will not be bound.

If you are using interlining, sew the side seams of the lining, then sew the side seams of the interlining separately and press seams open. With wrong sides together, baste the outer edges of the lining to the insulating layer using a narrow seam allowance no greater than ¼ in. Finish assembling the lining, including sewing in the sleeves.

Finish the hem by turning up the hem allowance and topstitching or blindstitching in place. Another option is to bind the bottom hem instead of hemming it. Next, finish the outside edge by overlocking and pressing back a ³⁄₈-in. seam allowance, or by binding the front edge with a Hong Kong finish if the lining fabric is bulky.

Finish the sleeves by turning up and machine-stitching the sleeve hems. To keep the sleeves in place at the bottom, attach an elastic loop to the hem at the underarm seam and sew a button onto the inside sleeve hem.

For coats with back vents, mark a cutting line the same height as the vent and staystitch along each side, tapering to the dot at the top, then cut along the cutting line.

Adding a back vent to the zip-out lining

When making a zip-out lining for a coat that has a back vent, begin by marking a cutting line at the center back of the assembled zip-out lining that is the same height as the vent. Mark a dot at the top of the vent, then draw a sewing line up one side of the cutting line and down the other. The sewing line should be ¼ in. from the cutting line at the hem and taper to the dot at the top. Next, staystitch along the sewing line, starting at the hem and sewing one or two stitches across the dot, pivoting twice and ending at the hem. Cut along the cutting line between the staystitching to the point.

Using a Hong Kong finish, bind the edges of the vent. The seam allowance on the vent follows the staystitching line, which is ¼ in. wide at the hem but very close to the cutting line at the point, while the seam allowance

on the bias binding is ¼ in. Pin the bias binding to the vent opening with right sides facing, then sew with the lining on top so you can stitch on top of the staystitching or just next to it farther in from the edge. If the coat has enough walking room, you may omit the center back opening on the zip-out lining.

Attaching the facing/lining unit to the coat

After the zip-out lining is prepared, try on all of the coat layers to make sure everything fits properly. If there is enough room, permanently sew the coat shoulder and side seams using the 1-in. seam allowance. If necessary, you could also take a smaller seam allowance.

To attach the facing/lining unit to the coat, pin and sew the unit to the outer edge of the coat with right sides together. Grade and press the seam open, then turn right side out and press the outer edge with wrong sides together. Sew the coat and sleeve hems using a blind catch-stitch, then finish sewing the permanent lining using a free-hanging hem (see pp. 53-54), the modified hand method (see pp. 33-37), or by bagging the lining (see pp. 37-39).

If you are bagging the lining, turn back the lining hem to line up with the raw edges of the coat hem at the front facings, then finish sewing the lining to the front facings, stopping at the bottom of the hem fold.

Finishing the zipper

With the zipper closed, place marks on the zipper tape at the center back, shoulder seams, or raglan sleeve seams. Also match up the zip-out lining to the facing edge and mark both zipper ends onto the front edges of the zip-out lining. Doing this will help you match the zipper to the zip-out lining in vital areas.

Next, separate the zipper and place the half that was not sewn to the facing under the outer edge of the zip-out lining, lining up the matchpoints and the edge to the zipper teeth. Stitch on top of the binding and close to the teeth. If you have overlocked and turned back the lining edge, start and end the stitch line at the lower front edges.

Just as is done in ready-to-wear coats, the zipper does not have to be as long as the lining edge. The bound or turned and stitched edge of the lining will simply hang down below the zipper area. On my sample garment, I kept the zip-out lining tucked beneath the flange created by the zipper application. To keep the lining's front edges tucked in place, add a small button to the back side of the zip-out lining and insert an elastic loop in the facing seam between the permanent lining and the facing.

If you bind the edges of the coat vent with a Hong Kong finish, miter the top for a professional look.

With the lining and the zipper facing up, line up the folded edge of the lining with the teeth of the zipper and stitch close to the teeth.

4 Vest linings

Lined vests are easier to sew than unlined vests and are much more comfortable to wear. The two ways of lining a vest are by using the quick lining method, where a vest is lined to the edge, or the classic lining method, where facings are used with a lining to finish the inside. By using the quick lining method, you can simplify the construction by eliminating the facings. Or you can use the classic lining application to create a beautifully tailored vest. The method you select depends on the fabric you use and the style of the vest you are sewing.

Men's vests typically combine the two techniques by using the classic lining application on the vest front and self-lining the back. This gives you the benefits of both methods by combining a nicely tailored front with a simplified back. This combination also works well on women's vests or any time you use lining fabric for the vest back.

In this chapter, I'll discuss how to choose which method to use and how to make a lining pattern based on each. I'll also show you how to construct the vest and insert the lining using the quick method, the classic method, and a combination of the two.

Selecting a Lining Method

Before lining a vest, you must decide whether to use the quick lining method or the classic lining method. The quick method lines the vest to the edge and works best when using lightweight to medium-weight stable fabrics with a similar hand. Use the quick lining method when self-lining or when you want to simplify the vest construction. When using this method, choose garment and lining fabrics that are the same or compatible because this method does not accommodate a back pleat or jump hem. For example, combine linen with linen, cotton with cotton, or combine linen with cotton if they have the same drape.

To use the classic lining method, the vest must have facings and a standard hem allowance or hem facing about 2 in. wide. This method should be used if you are combining a stretchy fashion fabric with a rigid lining layer or vice versa. Because differences in the fabrics cause problems such as pulling at the hem or deformities to the shape, this method uses a back pleat and jump hem to allow for variations in the fabric layers. You can also use this technique when self-lining is not feasible, such as when the fashion fabric is thick or has a nap like velvet or corduroy.

This method works best on tailored vests because using a facing and lining combination to finish the inside of the vest produces more tailored results. The best lining fabric choices for the classic lining method are rayon or polyester sheath lining, china silk, silky jacquards, or cotton batiste.

Making a Vest Lining Pattern

If you are using the quick lining method, there is no need to create a lining pattern; simply use the vest pattern to cut the lining the same as the outer vest

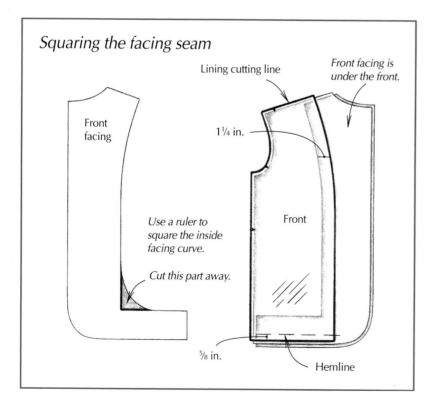

Squaring the facing seam

Lining cutting line

Front facing is under the front.

Front facing

1¼ in.

Use a ruler to square the inside facing curve.

Cut this part away.

Front

⅝ in.

Hemline

layer, making allowances for turn of cloth as you sew.

If you are using the classic lining method, the lining pattern will vary according to the vest's shape and type of hem. On some vests the lower edge may come to a point, while on others it may curve toward the side seam or be straight. On vests with contour edges, the front facing is often combined with a hem facing.

To create a classic vest lining pattern, position the front facing pattern beneath the front vest pattern, lining up the outer edges, and draw the lining cutting line 1¼ in. from the facing's inner edge. When the hem facing measures an equal distance from the bottom cutting line across the lower edge to the front facing, cut the lining length to be the same as the vest cutting length. An example of this is the curved front facing (see the illustration on the facing page). In this case, squaring the inside curve of the facing makes it easier to install the lining. Do this by using a ruler or an L square to mark the square inside corner, then cutting away the inside curve.

On a pointed vest, the hem facing may also be a consistent width from the bottom edge. If so, mark the lining cutting length the same as the vest cutting length. Sometimes the hem facing is a different size at the side seam than near the front

facings. In this case, measure the distance between the hem facing's inner edge and the hem cutting line at the side seam, then cut the lining length the same distance from the facing's inner edge across to the front facing (see the illustration below).

To simplify construction, eliminate any armhole facings by bringing the lining to the armhole edge. If the vest has a back neck facing, position the facing under the back vest pattern, lining up the neck edge, and mark the lining cutting line 1¼ in. from the facing's inner edge. Cut the lining length ⅝ in. below the finished vest length, and add a back pleat when

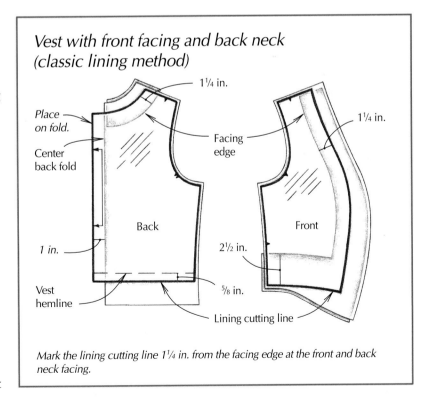

Vest with front facing and back neck (classic lining method)

Mark the lining cutting line 1¼ in. from the facing edge at the front and back neck facing.

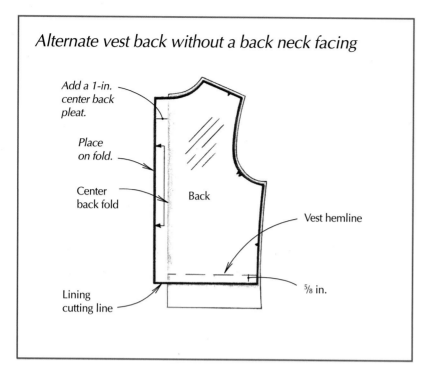

Alternate vest back without a back neck facing

Add a 1-in. center back pleat.

Place on fold.

Center back fold

Back

Vest hemline

Lining cutting line

5/8 in.

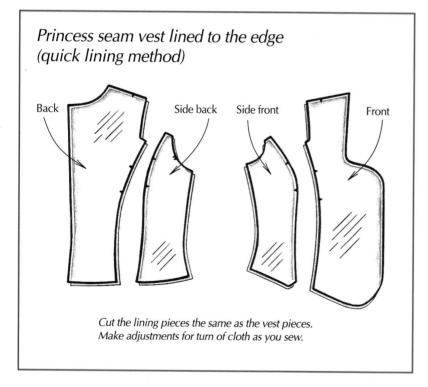

Princess seam vest lined to the edge (quick lining method)

Back

Side back

Side front

Front

Cut the lining pieces the same as the vest pieces.
Make adjustments for turn of cloth as you sew.

cutting by placing the center back 1 in. from the folded lining fabric. If the vest does not have a back neck facing, cut the back lining the same as the vest back, making the back pleat and length adjustments only (see the top illustration at left).

The vest front may have a hem allowance instead of a hem facing. In this case, the vest front lining adjustment is the same as the basic jacket front lining adjustment but omits the shoulder slope change.

Vests with princess seams may be lined to the edge using the quick lining method (see the bottom illustration at left) or lined using the classic method, whereby the facings are retained (see the top illustration on the facing page). The front pattern also serves as a front facing pattern, so cut four fronts out of vest fabric and use one pair as the facings. Adjust the side front, side back, and back patterns by making the lining cutting length 5/8 in. longer than the finished vest length. Also add the center back pleat to the back lining by cutting 1 in. in from the fabric fold.

Another lining option that you see in men's vests uses the classic lining for the vest front in combination with a self-lined back. In this case, use the classic lining adjustment for the front

Princess seam vest with front facing (classic lining method)

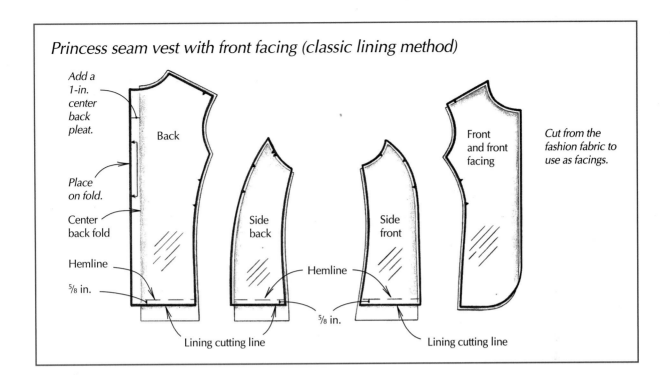

Add a 1-in. center back pleat.

Back

Place on fold.

Center back fold

Hemline

5/8 in.

Lining cutting line

Side back

Hemline

5/8 in.

Side front

Lining cutting line

Front and front facing

Cut from the fashion fabric to use as facings.

---

vest lining and cut the back lining the same as the vest back using a 5/8-in. hem allowance (see the illustration at right).

Constructing and Inserting a Vest Lining

The following instructions allow for variations in the design of the vest you are sewing. The vest may have one or all of the details depending on the complexity of the design, so follow just the steps that apply to the vest you are sewing.

Alternate vest back for self-lining

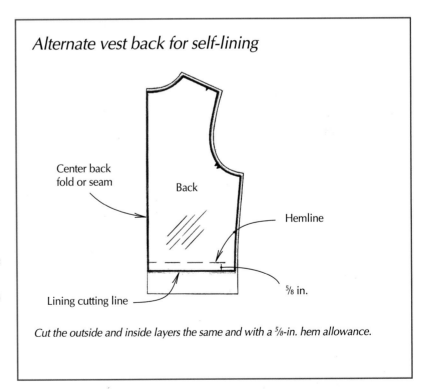

Center back fold or seam

Back

Hemline

Lining cutting line

5/8 in.

Cut the outside and inside layers the same and with a 5/8-in. hem allowance.

For a quick lining, connect the vest front to the vest back at the shoulders only. The vest lining is assembled the same way as the vest.

Sew the vest and lining front and neck edges together with right sides facing.

Preparing the vest

Begin preparing the vest by marking any dots, darts, and other matchpoints, then sew the darts, princess seams, and pockets or welts on the vest front. On the vest back, sew the center back seam, darts, and princess seams. Sew and connect the belt if there is one, then sew the front to the back at the shoulders and press the seams open. Press front darts toward the center front and back darts toward the center back.

Using the quick lining method

Begin by assembling the lining in the same manner as the vest. To attach the lining to the vest, pin along the front and neckline

edges with right sides together, then stitch those edges with a continuous seam. When the front edge curves into the front hem, stitch a few inches past the curve at the lower front. Trim or grade the seams and clip the curves, then press the seam allowances toward the lining and understitch. If your vest has points, cut the seam allowance diagonally after stitching the corners. Turn the vest right side out and press the seam so the lining is set back slightly from the front edge.

Understitching the front edge usually causes the lining edges to shift beyond the vest edges at the armholes and side seams. If this happens, trim the lining to be the same width as the vest at those areas. A thick fabric will

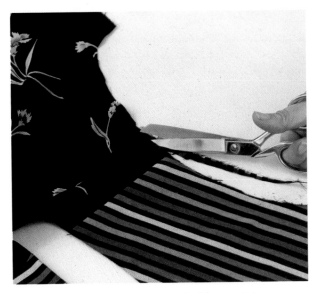

Trim the lining edge that has shifted beyond the vest edge at the armholes and possibly at the side seams to be the same width.

Reaching up through the back of the vest, turn the vest right side out by pulling the fronts through the shoulders.

shift a greater distance than a thin fabric.

Turn the vest right sides together again, then pin and stitch both armhole edges. Trim or grade the seam allowances, clip the curves, and press the seams flat then toward the lining. Turn the vest right side out by pulling the fronts of the vest through the shoulders to the back.

Lifting the lining away from the vest, pin the front vest to the back vest and the front lining to the back lining at the side seams with right sides together. Stitch the side seams of the vest and lining with one continuous stitch, leaving a 6-in. opening at one side seam to turn the vest right side out. Another option is to leave a 6-in. opening at the

Understitch the armholes as far as possible to keep the lining from rolling to the outside. Pulling the lining and vest fabric away from the seam as you understitch the armhole shrinks the length of the seam and reduces stretching at the underarm.

At the lower edge, slip a piece of fusible web into the opening and press it closed.

For a classic lining, press both the vest and the assembled lining before sewing them together.

side back along the lower edge. Press the side seams open. Understitch the armholes, starting as close as possible to the shoulder seam and continuing around to the other side, then press the armhole edge.

With right sides together, pin and stitch the remaining lower edge. Trim or grade the seam allowances, clip the curves, cut the corners diagonally, and press flat. Turn the vest right side out through either the side opening or the hem opening and press the lower edge. Edgestitch, slipstitch, or use fusible web to close the opening. Finally, make buttonholes and sew on buttons.

Using the classic lining method

The classic method for lining the vest follows the same sewing order as that for the quick method with a few additional steps to allow for the back pleat and jump hem. After preparing the vest, begin assembling the lining sections by pinning and sewing the facing to the lining, stopping 4 in. from the lower edge. Press the seam allowances toward the lining and sew any darts or princess seams.

For the back lining, make the back pleat by stitching along the marked lines with right sides together. Stitch for about 2 in. at the upper and lower edges and at the waist if you are sewing a long vest. After pressing the pleat flat,

then to one side, baste across the upper and lower edges to hold it in place. If the vest has a back neck facing, staystitch the back lining neckline and sew the lining to the back neck facing. Next, sew the front facing/lining to the back lining at the shoulders and press the seams open.

To attach the lining to the vest, follow the instructions for the quick lining method until you are ready to finish the lower edge. Leave the 6-in. opening to turn the vest right side out in the middle of one of the lining side seams. Next, turn up the vest hem on the hemline and press. Using a blind catchstitch, hand-sew close to the lower hem fold. If you don't want to hand-sew, topstitch the entire hem and front garment edge, starting at a side seam and using a continuous stitch around.

At the front facings, fold the raw edges of the lining and vest hems so that they line up, and finish stitching the seam, stopping at the fold. Press the seam allowances toward the lining.

To sew the vest and lining hems, pin the vest hem to the lining hem with right sides together, then sew, getting as close as possible to the front facings. Press the seam flat and pull the vest right side out through the side seam opening, then press the extra lining, which is the jump hem, toward the bottom to form a crease.

Sewing a classic front lining with a self-lined back

Using the classic lining method for the vest front and self-lining the back is your best choice when you want to use the lining fabric for the vest back. You typically see this combination on men's vests, where the front is nicely tailored while the back is kept simple.

To sew a vest using this method, begin by pinning and sewing each front lining to each front facing along the facing seam with right sides together. Fold up the raw edge of the lining hem to line up with the upper raw edge of the hem facing, then cut away the triangle of lining hem that extends past the front edge. You only have to make this adjustment when the lining hem meets the facing seam at a sharp angle that is less than 90°. Press the seam flat, then press the seam allowances toward the lining.

Next, sew the lining hem to the facings' upper edge with right sides together, getting as close as possible to the front facing. Press the extra lining or jump hem toward the bottom facing to form a crease, then baste the crease to the hem facing at the side seam using a ¼-in. seam allowance.

Compare the lengths of the vest side seam and the side seam on the lining/facing unit to make sure they are equal. If there is

After folding and pinning the lining hem to line up with the vest hem at the lower front edge, cut away the lining hem allowance that extends past the front lining edge.

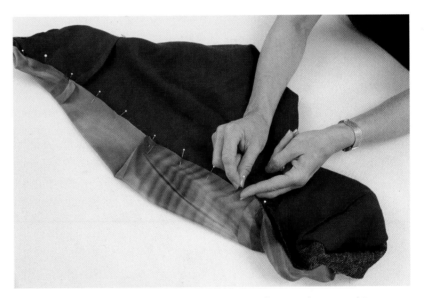

Pin the vest hem to the lining hem with right sides together, matching all seams.

any difference, adjust the size of the jump hem before basting at the side seam.

Now treat this facing/lining unit as a simple lining front and follow the directions for quick lining the vest.

5 Skirt Linings

I line all close-fitting, straight, or A-line skirts because the lining creates a smooth silhouette that doesn't cling. Full skirts that are gathered or pleated at the waist and circular skirts do not necessarily need a lining, but you may want to add one to support the fashion fabric or if the fashion fabric is sheer.

Appropriate lining fabrics include rayon or polyester sheath lining, china silk, cotton or poly-cotton batiste or broadcloth, and blouseweight microfiber. Silk or polyester crepe de Chine, charmeuse, and jacquards are also good. You should select the lining fabric that is most compatible with the weight of the fashion fabric and how it will be cleaned. I prefer skirt linings that slide easily but do not wrinkle, so that limits my choices to polyester sheath lining, lightweight microfiber, polyester crepe de Chine, charmeuse, and jacquards. For skirts that will be worn in warm weather, rayon, cotton, and silk linings are more comfortable to wear next to the skin.

In this chapter, I will show you how to make a full skirt lining pattern, as well as patterns for skirts with waist facings, pleated skirts, and skirts with partial linings. I'll discuss how to construct and insert a full or partial lining and how to underline a skirt. Finally, I'll explain how to finish your skirt, including finishing the zipper area and the lining hems.

Making a Skirt Lining Pattern

To make a skirt lining pattern, use the main skirt pattern pieces excluding the waistband, facings, and inseam pockets. Eliminate the inseam pocket extension along the side seams since inseam pockets do not influence the lining application. If the skirt has slanted pockets, pin the pocket pattern behind the pocket opening to complete the front pattern. Adjust the lining cutting length to be ⅝ in. longer than the finished skirt length (see the illustration below).

Skirt with waist facings

When a skirt has waist facings instead of a waistband, you may cut the lining to start where the facing ends. Make pattern adjustments by placing the waist facing pattern under the front and back skirt patterns, aligning the upper edges. You will need to fold out the darts or pleats by matching up the sewing lines on darts or foldlines on pleats. Draw the upper lining cutting line 1¼ in. from the facing edge toward the waist, then adjust the lining cutting length to be ⅝ in. longer than the finished skirt length (see the illustration on the facing page).

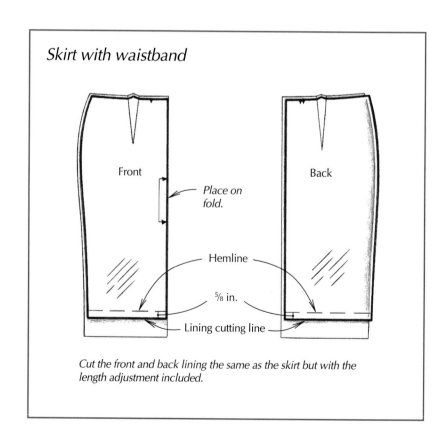

Skirt with waistband

Front

Place on fold.

Back

Hemline

⅝ in.

Lining cutting line

Cut the front and back lining the same as the skirt but with the length adjustment included.

If you will be using the quick lining method for a skirt with waist facings (see pp. 80-81), cut the lining the same as the skirt, making only the length adjustment.

Pleated skirt

The lining to a pleated skirt will either have a straight or an A-line shape. This is one of the few occasions where I make a separate lining pattern so as not to pleat the garment pattern every time I reuse it. To make the lining pattern, bring the foldlines of the pleats together, using pins or removable tape to hold them in place. One or more pleats

usually have hidden darts between the hips and waistline. If you force these foldlines together, the pattern will curve. Match the foldlines starting at the bottom of the skirt, and pin just to the point where the pattern remains flat. The pleat sewing lines will separate more as they reach the waist, forming a dart.

After placing pattern tissue over the pleated skirt pattern, copy the outer edges and mark the darts that form at the waist onto the lining pattern (see the illustration on p. 78). Because the darts will be on the inside, it doesn't matter if they are longer than you'd expect. Adjust the

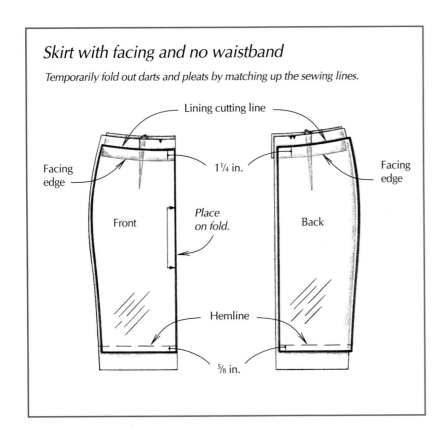

Skirt with facing and no waistband

Temporarily fold out darts and pleats by matching up the sewing lines.

Lining cutting line

Facing edge

1¼ in.

Facing edge

Front

Place on fold.

Back

Hemline

⅝ in.

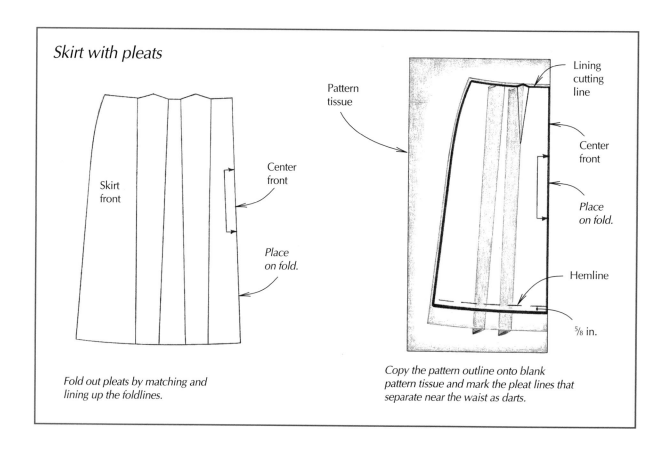

Skirt with pleats

Skirt front

Center front

Place on fold.

Fold out pleats by matching and lining up the foldlines.

Pattern tissue

Lining cutting line

Center front

Place on fold.

Hemline

⅝ in.

Copy the pattern outline onto blank pattern tissue and mark the pleat lines that separate near the waist as darts.

lining length to be ⅝ in. longer than the length of the finished skirt. If the lining pattern is narrow at the bottom, add a slit at the center back seam or both side seams. Leave the seam unstitched starting about 6 in. above the knee. Hold the pattern up against the body to mark where the slit begins, then press the seams twice and stitch.

Partial skirt lining

If you choose to use a partial lining, cut the lining using the skirt pattern so it ends 1 in. below the upper seam of the vent opening or below the seat if

there is no vent. Change the lengthwise grain using a triangle or L square, and mark the new grain perpendicular to the old one (see the illustration on the facing page). When you cut the lining, place the bottom cutting line along the fabric's selvage so you won't have to hem it.

Constructing and Inserting a Skirt Lining

The most common way to line skirts is to use a full lining that is connected at the waistband and

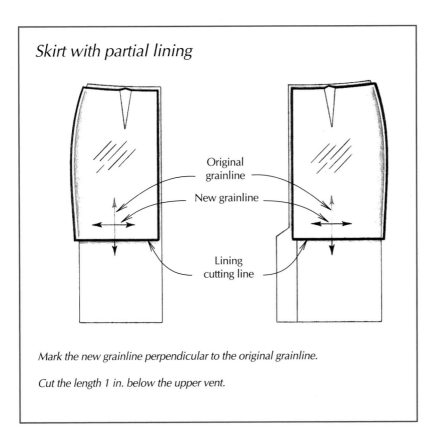

Skirt with partial lining

Original grainline

New grainline

Lining cutting line

Mark the new grainline perpendicular to the original grainline.

Cut the length 1 in. below the upper vent.

hemmed separately from the skirt. Other skirt styles have waist facings instead of a waistband. Sometimes a partial lining is the best solution to lining the skirt where the lining does the most good while keeping the skirt lightweight and cool. Some skirt styles or fabrics are good candidates for underlining, which stabilizes the fashion fabric and makes it opaque.

Full skirt lining

Using a full lining is the most common way to line a skirt and is relatively easy to do, especially on a straight or A-line skirt. An advantage to a full lining is that it eliminates the need to wear a slip.

To prepare the skirt, sew the skirt together including any darts, pleats, zipper, and pockets. Press the front darts toward the center front and back darts toward the center back, then press the pleats according to the pattern directions. The lining will need to be attached before adding the waistband and hemming the skirt.

When you sew the lining, lengthen the zipper opening by

If you want to simplify sewing the lining, convert the darts to pleats as you pin the lining to the skirt waist seam. Pin with wrong sides together, matching the center front, side seams, and center back. Fold out the excess lining next to each dart equal to the depth of the dart and pin. Then baste the waist seam using a $\frac{1}{2}$-in. seam allowance.

sewing the zipper to $\frac{1}{2}$ in. to 1 in. below the zipper dot and back-stitching. Next, sew the rest of the lining together, including darts. Press the lining darts in the opposite direction of the skirt darts or toward the side seams.

The next step is to finish the zipper area according to one of the methods on pp. 86-88. Then attach the lining to the skirt by machine-basting the wrong side of the lining to the wrong side of the skirt at the waist seam using a $\frac{1}{2}$-in. seam allowance. Attach the waistband to the skirt to enclose the waist seam following the pattern directions or using your favorite method.

Finish the skirt's hem edge using a zigzag stitch, a machine or serger overlock stitch, rayon or lace seam binding, or a Hong Kong finish. Hem the skirt by hand using a blind catchstitch or by machine using a blindstitch, then hem the lining 1 in. shorter than the skirt using a topstitch.

Quick lining a skirt with waist facings

My favorite way to line skirts with waist facings is using the quick lining method. The traditional way of lining skirts with waist facings is to connect the lining to the lower edge of the interfaced facing. The quick lining method gives you the same look but eliminates the need for interfacing. The lining layer goes to the waist edge

under the facing layer, therefore the lining serves as interfacing.

Begin by cutting the waist facings using the facing patterns. Turn the lower seam allowance under and press but don't sew the lower edge. It is easier to press curved edges if you staystitch $\frac{1}{4}$ in. from the edge and use the stitch as the guide for pressing under the seam allowance.

Once the facings are prepared, cut the lining using the garment pattern, then sew the lining, including darts, pleats, and the center back seam but not the side seams. Sew the seam leading to the zipper, stopping $\frac{1}{2}$ in. to 1 in. below the zipper mark. Press darts and pleats in the opposite direction as those on the skirt and press seams open.

To attach the facings to the lining, place the wrong side of the facings on top of the right side of the lining. Machine-baste the raw edges using a $\frac{1}{2}$-in. seam allowance, then edgestitch the folded facing edge to the lining. Sew the facing/lining unit side seams and press them open.

To attach the lining, pin and stitch to the skirt waist seam with right sides together, then trim or grade the waist seam, clipping if necessary. Trimming the parts of the seams that are enclosed in the waist seam cuts down on bulk in the waistline area. Understitch the waist seam,

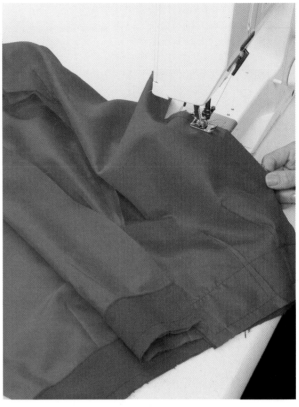

When sewing a quick lining for a skirt with waist facings, pressing the curved edge of the facing is easier if you staystitch first, then use the stitching as a guide.

After you have sewn the facings to the right side of the lining, sew the front and back together at the side seams with right sides facing.

then finish the zipper area and hem separately.

If the skirt has a raised waist and the fashion fabric is soft, you may want to interface the waist area anyway. Begin by either interfacing the facings as usual or interfacing the waist area of the fashion fabric. To do the latter, cut fusible interfacing using the facing pattern, then fuse the interfacing to the skirt waist instead of to the facings. Don't fuse over stitched darts or seams, but instead cut the interfacing apart where it aligns with the dart seam and fuse to both sides of the dart.

If you are using fashion fabric that is thick, you can eliminate the facings altogether and line to the waist seam. In this case, interface the upper edge of the lining using the facing pattern to cut the fusible interfacing.

Partial skirt lining

If you choose to use a partial skirt lining, cut the lining so it ends 1 in. below the upper seam of the vent opening or below the

To reduce bulk, trim and grade the waist seam before turning right side out. Trim away all dart and vertical seam allowances that fall within the waist seam without cutting the stitching.

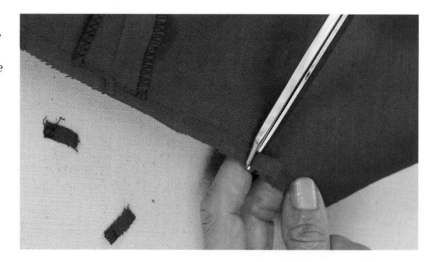

Understitch the waist facing to keep it from rolling toward the skirt side.

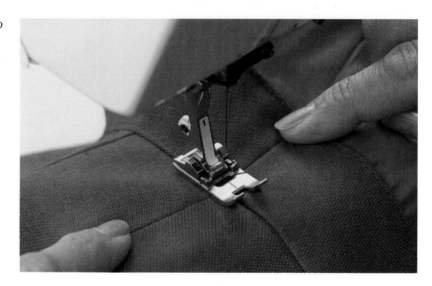

seat if there is no vent. You can avoid having to hem the lining by cutting it on the crossgrain and using the selvage as the finished edge. Otherwise, allow a 1-in. hem allowance, turning back the hem allowance ½ in. twice and stitching in place. Sew the partial lining together in the same manner as the full lining and attach it to the skirt just before attaching the waistband.

If you are lining just the skirt back, which cuts down on bagging in the seat area and is common on wrap skirts, cut the lining on the crossgrain using the back pattern piece. Sew any darts on the skirt back and on the back lining, then machine-baste the lining to the waist and side seams of the skirt back with wrong sides together using a ½-in. seam allowance. If the skirt has a center back seam and zipper, sew the center back seam of the skirt and lining separately so you end up with a neat finish. After basting the lining to the skirt side seams, treat them as one layer when you sew the skirt together.

Skirt underlining

If your skirt fabric is lightweight, loosely woven, or white or a pastel color, you can use an underlining to support the skirt fabric and make it more opaque. Underlining the skirt will also help to reduce stretching and wrinkling, while this underlining method finishes the seams as well. Good fabric choices for underlining include rayon or polyester sheath lining and cotton batiste.

The skirt underlining is attached to each skirt panel with right sides together before sewing the skirt together. If you plan to sew a lapped zipper, increase the seam allowance at the zipper opening of the skirt and under-lining by $3/8$ in. so there will be enough seam allowance to properly install the zipper.

There are two ways to handle darts and stitched-down pleats when you use underlining. The first way is to treat the skirt and underlining fabric as one when sewing the darts and pleats. This is a good method to use when making the fabric opaque because it prevents construction

details from showing through to the outside. It's also a good way to reinforce the details. To use this application, mark darts and other construction details on the right side of the underlining only, then sew darts and stitched-down pleats after attaching the underlining to the fashion fabric.

The second method, which I prefer because it has a more finished look, involves sewing the darts and stitched-down pleats on the skirt layer and on the underlining layer separately before attaching the underlining to the skirt. This application is best when underlining thick fabrics because sewing the darts on each layer separately is less bulky than treating the two layers as one.

To use this method, mark the darts and stitched-down pleats on the wrong side of both the skirt layer and the underlining layer. Although you may sew the darts and stitched-down pleats before or after adjusting the underlining for turn of cloth, it is more efficient to sew them first. Any unstitched pleats should be treated as one layer with the underlining.

Adjusting the underlining for turn of cloth After cutting the underlining the same as the skirt fabric, it is important to adjust the width of each underlining section to allow for turn of cloth because the underlining is handled together with the fashion fabric as it curves around the body. This adjustment gives the underlining a smaller circumference than the skirt as it goes around the body and results in a smoother fit.

To adjust for turn of cloth, position each underlining section on top of the corresponding skirt section with right sides together. Pin or baste along the center of each skirt section, then fold the sections along the center, folding the skirt around the underlining. Because this causes the underlining to extend past the fabric edges along the vertical seams, trim the excess underlining. There will be more to trim if the fashion fabric is thick.

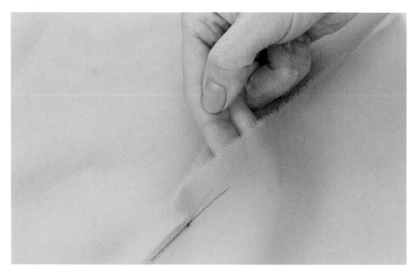

To line a sheer skirt, reinforce-stitch through the zipper mark of each skirt panel (shown here in contrasting thread), and clip the seam allowance. Sew the seam using an appropriate finish for sheer fabrics such as a French seam or a narrow double-stitched seam.

Attaching the underlining to the skirt

Before attaching the underlining to the skirt, sew the darts and stitched-down pleats in the skirt layer and in the underlining layer if you are using the second method.

Next, clean-finish the vertical seams by pinning the corresponding skirt and underlining sections with right sides together and sewing them using a ⅛-in. seam allowance. It is usually easier to sew seams with the underlining facing up because the underlining fabric tends to be more stable and tightly woven than the fashion fabric. Be sure to keep the edges together to avoid missing the bottom layer in some spots or changing the turn-of-cloth adjustment. Without sewing the waist and hem yet, press seams open or toward the underlining, then turn the skirt right side out. Press seams along the edge.

You can attach the underlining to the fashion fabric using a seam allowance up to ¼ in. wide. I increase the width of the seam allowance if the fashion fabric is thick or frays easily. When you increase the seam allowance used to attach the underlining to the skirt, you must decrease the seam allowance used to sew the skirt.

Sewing the skirt/underlining unit

The fashion fabric and underlining should now be treated as one. Baste along the waist edge using a ½-in. seam allowance and through the center of each dart and pleat, going 1 in. past the end marks. Next, sew the darts and stitched-down pleats if you're using the first method, then sew the skirt together, install the zipper, and attach the waistband. Sew the finished seams using a ½-in. seam allowance. If you attached the underlining using a ¼-in. seam allowance, then sew the skirt together using a ⅜-in. seam allowance.

Hemming the skirt To hem the skirt, baste the fashion fabric and underlining along the hemline and fold back the hem. Adjust the hem allowance to allow for turn of cloth and trim away any underlining that extends past the hem edge. Finish the hem edge using seam binding, a Hong Kong finish, or your favorite method and hem the skirt.

Sheer skirt lining

The lining on sheer skirts is treated differently than on other skirts so that the seam allowances and zipper don't show through. Begin by reinforce-stitching through the zipper mark on each skirt panel. Clip the seam allowance to the mark.

Sew the skirt together using an appropriate seam for sheer fabrics, such as a narrow French seam or a narrow overlock stitch, but leave the zipper opening unfinished. Then sew the lining together using an appropriate

seam finish. The lining seam could simply be pressed open or pressed open and edge-finished with a narrow zigzag stitch or an overlock stitch. If you plan to use a French seam or serge the lining seams together, you must also reinforce-stitch the lining through the zipper mark, and clip to the zipper mark as you did on the skirt. Then you can use the French seam or overlock below the zipper.

To attach the lining to the skirt, pin the wrong side of the skirt to the right side of the lining, making sure the upper edges and the zipper opening are even. Baste the waist seam using a ½-in. seam allowance. At the zipper opening, baste the raw edges together using a ½-in.

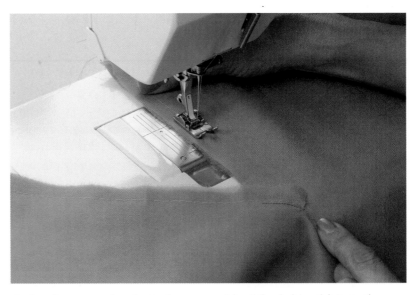

At the zipper opening, baste the wrong side of the fashion fabric to the right side of the lining using a ½-in. seam allowance. Treat the two layers as one to insert the zipper.

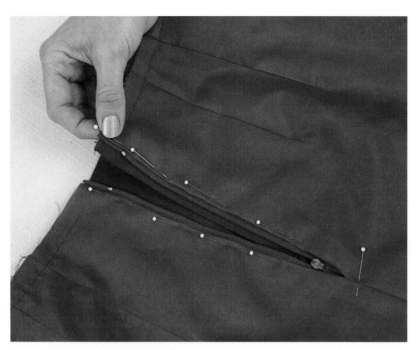

When attaching the lining to the zipper tape by hand, leave enough room so the lining does not interfere with opening and closing the zipper.

the following applications you need to leave the lining zipper opening ½ in. to 1 in. longer than the garment zipper opening.

Attaching the lining to zipper tape by hand

To attach the lining to the zipper tape by hand, pin the wrong side of the lining to the wrong side of the skirt at the waist. Fold the lining under next to the zipper teeth, pin in place, but allow easy opening and closing of the zipper by not getting too close to the teeth. Next, machine-baste the waist seam using a ½-in. seam allowance. Pin then slipstitch the lining to the zipper tape.

Attaching the lining to zipper tape by machine

Attaching the lining to the zipper tape can be done with either an invisible zipper or a standard zipper.

Using an invisible zipper

Invisible zippers are easy to finish. The invisible zipper seam pulls away from the outside layer, making it easy to machine-sew the lining along the zipper tape using a zipper foot. At the zipper opening, pin the lining to the skirt with right sides together, sandwiching the zipper between the layers. Avoiding sewing too close to the zipper teeth, stitch the layers, catching the outer edge of the zipper tape using a

seam allowance, then edge-finish the zipper opening using a narrow zigzag stitch or a machine or serger overlock stitch. Treating the skirt and lining as one layer, install the zipper.

Finishing the Zipper Area

There are several ways to finish the zipper area in skirts, pants, dresses, jackets, and any place you may have a zipper and a lining. You can connect the lining to the zipper tape by hand or machine, or you can hem the edges of the lining, leaving the lining free from the zipper. You should select the method that best suits your taste and skill level. Remember that for all of conventional zipper foot. Stop sewing near the bottom of the zipper opening. If either the fashion fabric or the lining fabric is on the bias or a knit, machine-baste first, then turn right side out to check for stretching. After sewing the zipper opening, machine-baste the wrong side of the lining to the wrong side of the skirt at the waist using a ½-in. seam allowance.

Using a standard zipper To connect the lining to a standard zipper, begin by machine-basting the wrong side of the lining to the wrong side of the skirt at the waist using a ½-in. seam allowance and stopping 1 in. from each side of the zipper tape. Fold back the lining seam allowance on top of the zipper tape about ¼ in. from the zipper teeth and hold in place using pins or ⅛-in. double-sided basting tape. Reach between the layers, repin the seam allowances, and stitch the edge of the skirt seam allowance to the lining seam allowance using a zipper foot. Note that the edges will not line up because the lining has been folded to clear the zipper teeth.

Finishing the lining without attaching it to the zipper

The easiest way to finish the lining edge at the zipper opening is by stitching a narrow machine-stitched hem and leaving the

To machine-sew a lining to an invisible zipper, pin and stitch the lining, outer edge of the zipper tape, and skirt together, avoiding getting too close to the zipper teeth.

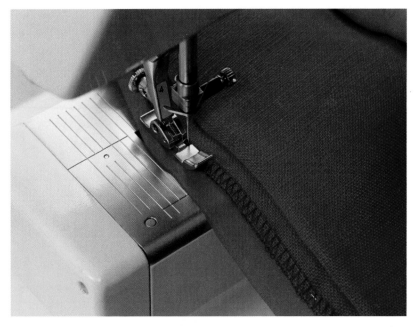

For a standard zipper, after repinning between the layers, machine-sew the lining to the seam allowance at the zipper opening using the zipper foot. The raw edges will not match up.

To finish the zipper opening, turn and press the raw edges of the lining to meet the foldline. Pinning the upper edge to the ironing board makes it easy to hold the lining in place as you press a fold.

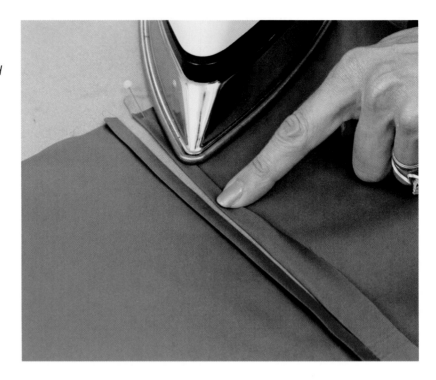

lining and zipper unattached. After leaving the lining opening ½ in. to 1 in. longer than the skirt opening, press the seam open and press back the ⅝-in. seam allowance at the zipper opening. Then fold back and press the raw edges to meet the foldline.

Stitch close to the second fold. Start sewing from the waist downward, then pivot at the bottom of the opening, sew across the bottom, pivot again, and sew the other side to the waist. Machine-baste the wrong side of the lining to the wrong side of the skirt at the waist using a ½-in. seam allowance.

Lining hems

The skirt lining hem can be stitched quickly and easily by machine. You can either leave the lining hem free-hanging or connect it to the skirt hem.

Using a free-hanging lining hem

Using a free-hanging lining hem is the best and easiest way to hem skirts and dresses, particularly those with side or back vents and skirts that flare at the hem. When using this method, the lining and skirt should be hemmed individually. To hem a straight or A-line skirt, you'll need a 2-in. to 3-in. hem allowance. Finish the skirt hem by pressing it back and using an edge finish, rayon or lace seam binding, or a Hong Kong finish to neaten the raw edges. Finish the lining hem to be 1 in. shorter than the skirt length. To do this, turn back the lining hem allowance twice and stitch close to the first fold. For example, if you have a 1½-in. hem allowance, press back ¾ in. twice and stitch close to the upper fold. Start sewing the lining hem at the vent opening, at a side seam, or at the center back seam, keeping the fabric taut as you sew.

Adding a lace edge to the bottom of the skirt lining is a nice touch. Instead of turning up the hem, sew the upper edge of the lace trim with a straight stitch on top of the lining so that the lower edge is 1 in. above the finished skirt hem. Cut away the lining fabric behind the trim to leave a ¼-in. seam allowance, then press the seam allowance away from the lace and stitch the lace edge again from the top, catching the seam allowance. For this step, use a narrow zigzag stitch setting of 2 for the width and length.

Hemming flared skirts Skirts and dresses that flare at the bottom look best with a small hem allowance to avoid the excess ease that results from pressing up a wide hem. A circular hem, which is the most extreme example of a hem that flares, needs to be small, no more than 1 in. wide. Before hemming circular and off-grain skirts, allow both the skirt and lining to stretch.

To do this, pin the waistline to a hanger, keeping the waistline straight, and wait a minimum of 24 hours before remarking the hem. When marking the new hem, put the skirt on and measure the same distance up from the floor to make the hemline even.

Hem the skirt according to the pattern directions or use a narrow turned and stitched hem. To do this, stitch ¼ in. from the raw edge using easestitch plus (see the sidebar on p. 90), then turn the hem back and press along the stitching line. Turn the hem back again and press, keeping the hem about ⅜ in. wide, then stitch close to the first fold.

Cut the lining hem to be ⅜ in. shorter than the finished skirt length to give you a ⅝-in. hem allowance on the lining. Finish the lining hem using a narrow turned and stitched hem or on the serger using a rolled hem.

USES FOR EASESTITCH PLUS AND STAYSTITCH PLUS

To simplify sewing a skirt lining, you can convert darts to ease or pleats along the waist seam. Use a technique called easestitch plus to reduce the fullness at the waist seam. To do this, machine-sew along the lining waist seam, using your finger to apply pressure behind the presser foot (see the photo at right). This forces extra fabric into each stitch, thus reducing the size of the waist seam.

The eased lining waist seam should be the same size as the skirt waist seam after the darts are stitched. If you have eased too much, cut a few stitches to increase the size of the lining. If the lining is too big, sew again with easestitch plus next to the first row.

Many skirt waist seams must be eased into the waistband. You can use easestitch plus when sewing the lining to the skirt at the waist seam, easing both layers together to reduce the size of the waist seam.

The same technique used for easestitch plus applies to staystitch plus, which is useful when pressing outside curves and circular hems. To use staystitch plus, apply pressure behind the presser foot and all along the hem as you sew ¼ in. from the edge. Doing this will shrink and stabilize the hem, making it easier to press back the raw edge. When staystitching facing edges, it is only necessary to apply pressure behind the presser foot on curves and on off-grain or bias areas such as those found on

both sides of the center front and center back on a neck facing. Sew one continuous stitch ¼ in. from the edge.

Staystitch plus also can be used to control stretching when attaching the facings or linings to sleeves or any type of garment. In these cases, apply pressure behind the presser foot in the areas most prone to stretching, which include the front and back of the lower armhole curves and scoop and V-necklines.

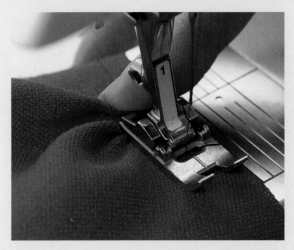

When using easestitch plus, the fabric will build up behind the presser foot and will have to be released every few inches.

Connecting the lining hem to the skirt hem

The lining hem can be attached to the skirt hem to completely enclose the inside layers. This method works best on skirts and dresses with straight side seams.

To connect the lining hem to the skirt hem by hand, press back the lining hem to be the same length as the skirt, and trim the lining hem allowance if it is greater than ⅝ in. Next, pin the folded edge of the lining so that it just covers the skirt hem edge and slipstitch. Smooth the excess lining toward the hem and gently steam the fold.

You can also connect the skirt hem to the lining hem by machine if you change the construction sequence of the skirt. To do this, sew the skirt together, including darts, pleats, zipper, and pockets, then press the seams and darts following the pattern instructions. Next, sew the lining together, including darts, and press. Press up the skirt hem and sew at least 1 in. below the cut edge, otherwise it would be difficult to machine-sew the lining.

Next, pin the lining hem to the skirt hem with right sides facing, aligning the cut edges, and stitch using a ⅝-in. seam allowance. Pull the lining into the skirt with wrong sides together, then finish the zipper area using one of the methods on pp. 86-88. Using a ½-in. seam allowance, machine-baste the wrong side of the lining to the wrong side of the skirt at the waist seam. Finally, attach the waistband to the skirt to enclose the waist seam using your favorite method.

To attach the lining to the skirt hem by hand, stitch the lining hem to the skirt hem with right sides facing and raw edges aligned.

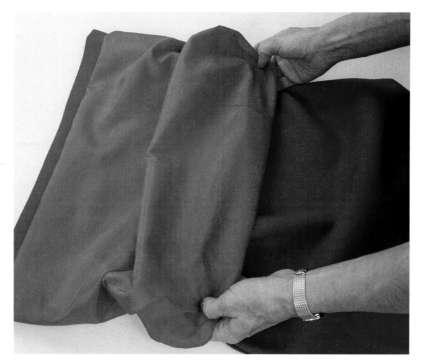

If you have attached the lining to the skirt hem by machine, pull the lining over the skirt with wrong sides facing.

6 Pants Linings

Without question, lined pants look better and are more comfortable to wear than unlined pants. Lined pants slide more easily when you move and have a smooth silhouette that is more flattering to the wearer. You can line all types of pants, including culottes, shorts, and elastic-waist styles.

The best lining fabric is tightly woven, smooth, durable, and lighter in weight than the fashion fabric. Cotton or poly-cotton batiste or broadcloth, rayon or polyester sheath lining, China silk, blouse-weight microfiber, silk or polyester crepe de Chine, charmeuse, and jacquards are all appropriate lining fabrics. You should select the lining fabric that is most compatible with the fashion fabric and how it will be cleaned. For example, if you are going to wash the pants, choose a washable lining that doesn't wrinkle much. Cotton, silk, and rayon, which are comfortable next to the body, especially in warm weather, can be used in washable pants, but expect to do some extra pressing. On the other hand, poly-cotton and polyester linings are washable and require little or no pressing. These are good lining choices for fashion fabrics that wrinkle because they help keep the outer layer smooth.

If you want to underline your pants, cotton or poly-cotton batiste and slippery lining fabrics are good choices. For best results, you should use an opaque underlining fabric when using the underlining technique described on pp. 104-105.

In this chapter, I will show you how to make a pants lining pattern, including how to adjust a pattern for a partial lining, for pants with waist facings, and for pants with a fly front closure. I will then discuss how to construct and insert a full lining, partial lining, and underlining.

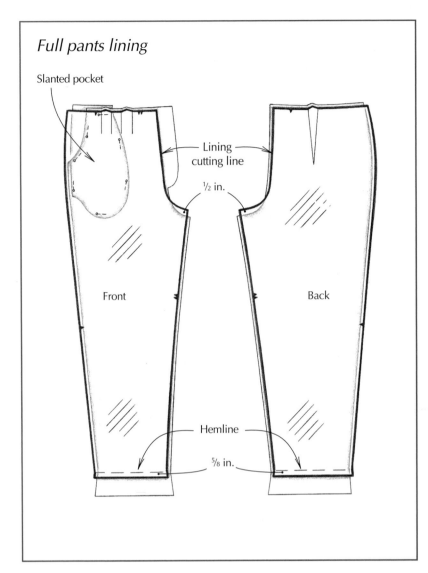

Full pants lining

Slanted pocket

Lining cutting line

½ in.

Front

Back

Hemline

⅝ in.

Making a Pants Lining Pattern

To make a full lining pattern, use the main pants pattern pieces excluding the waistband, facings, and pockets. Also eliminate the fly front extensions and in-seam pocket extensions. On pants with slanted pockets, the side front pocket pattern must be pinned to the front pattern section, matching the appropriate marks, but in-seam pockets should just be eliminated in the lining layer.

On the lining pattern, raise the crotch curve ½ in. at the inseam, blending to the original seam. You may also make this adjustment by sewing the crotch seam with a ¼-in. seam allowance near the inseam that blends to the ⅝-in. seam at each end of the crotch curve. Adjust the lining cutting length to be ⅝ in. longer than the finished pants length (see the illustration at left).

Partial pants lining

If you are making a partial lining, cut the lining using the pants front and back pattern pieces but end 5 in. below the knee (see the illustration at left on the facing page). You can avoid having to hem the lining by cutting it on the crossgrain so that the selvages serve as a finished hem. To keep the grain accurate, measure the grainline to a torn crosswise edge.

Partial pants lining

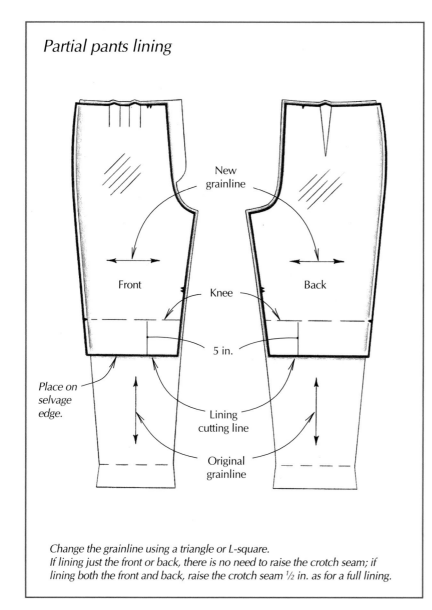

New
grainline

Front

Back

Knee

5 in.

Place on
selvage
edge.

Lining
cutting line

Original
grainline

Change the grainline using a triangle or L-square.
*If lining just the front or back, there is no need to raise the crotch seam; if
lining both the front and back, raise the crotch seam ½ in. as for a full lining.*

Pants lined only at knee

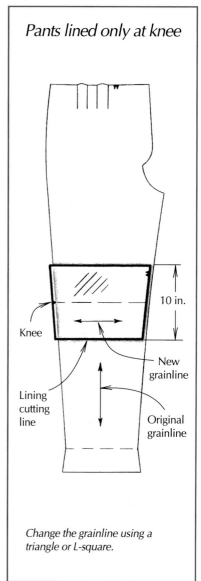

10 in.

Knee

New
grainline

Lining
cutting
line

Original
grainline

*Change the grainline using a
triangle or L-square.*

You may partially line both the front and back or just the front or just the back. To partially line both the front and back, raise the crotch curve as you would on a full lining and follow the same sewing directions. There is no need to raise the crotch seam if you are lining just the front or back.

Another partial lining option is to line the front knee area only to control stretching. In this case, cut the lining to extend 5 in. above and 5 in. below the knee area (see the illustration above right). Cut the lining on the crosswise grain, lining up the upper or lower edge to the selvage of the fabric.

For a quick lining on pants with waist facings, attach the wrong side of the facings on top of the right side of the lining, then sew the lining side seams. After pressing seams open, attach as a single unit to the pants as if attaching the facing. Pin and stitch the waist seam with right sides facing, then trim or grade it, clipping the curved areas. Understitch the waist seam, and select a zipper finishing method.

Pants lining with waist facings

If your pants have facings, use the traditional or quick lining method to cut the waist area of the lining (see the illustration on the facing page and pp. 76-78 for an explanation of the methods).

Pants lining with a fly front closure

The classic zipper application for pants is the fly front closure, whereby the zipper is not centered but extends or laps to the other side where you see the topstitching. There are many variations of the fly front closure. For example, men's pants have the fly stitching on the left, while

women's pants normally have the stitching on the right. The width of the underlap can range from ¼ in. to ½ in., and some patterns have a fly shield connecting to the zipper underlap and some do not.

The left and right lining will be different in the zipper area because of the zipper application and the fly facing. To make the lining pattern, adjust the pants pattern by folding back the fly front extension or fly facing at the center front along the marked foldline. Some patterns have a separate pattern piece for the fly facing. In this case, position the fly facing pattern underneath the pants pattern, aligning the matchpoints and edges.

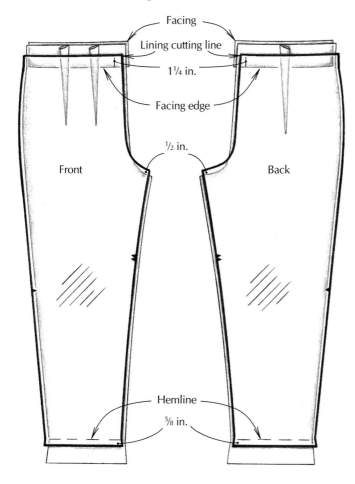

Pants with waist facings instead of a waistband

Facing

Lining cutting line

1¼ in.

Facing edge

½ in.

Front

Back

Hemline

⅝ in.

To mark the lining cutting line at the facing seam, temporarily fold out the darts and pleats by matching the sewing lines, then place the facing pattern beneath the pants pattern at the waist, lining up the edges. Mark the lining cutting line 1¼ in. beyond the facing's inner edge.

The inner edge of the fly facing is the reference point for marking the lining cutting line. Measure and mark the lining cutting line ¾ in. from the facing edge and use a seam allowance of ⅜ in. for attaching the lining to the fly facing. The smaller seamline makes it easier to sew around the curved seam and is less bulky.

Cut both lining fronts the same way, eliminating the fly front extension and leaving a ⅝-in. seam allowance past the center front fold. Mark the fly facing adjustment on both the left and right

Mark the fly facing adjustment on both the left and right lining fronts.

lining fronts. You will eventually cut away one side, depending on whether the fly front closure is stitched on the left or right front (see the top illustration on the facing page). The best way to avoid cutting away the wrong side of the lining is by stitching the lining together, leaving the zipper opening 1 in. longer than the garment opening, and cutting away the fly facing adjustment after aligning to the garment with wrong sides together.

You can simplify the lining application at the fly front closure by not connecting the lining to the zipper (see the bottom illustration on the facing page). Cut both fronts to allow for the placement of the zipper because it extends ¼ in. to ½ in. beyond the center front. Mark the front cutting line ⅝ in. from the zipper placement line at the waist and connect to the original ⅝-in. cutting line at the bottom of the fly opening.

Constructing and Inserting a Pants Lining

The lining application you select depends on the fashion fabric you use, the style of the garment, and the season. A full lining serves as the best barrier between a scratchy fabric and you, while a partial lining from the waist to just below the knee keeps the

pants lightweight and cool. Underlining is the best choice for fabrics that are semitransparent, loosely woven, or wrinkle-prone.

Full lining on pants with waistbands

A full lining completely encloses the inside construction details of the pants. The steps to follow for a full lining are to first prepare the pants, then sew and insert the lining, finishing the zipper area before basting the waist seams together and attaching the waistband. Finally, finish the lining hem by using a free-hanging hem or by connecting the lining hem to the pants hem by hand or machine.

Preparing the pants Sew the pants together, including darts, pleats, zipper, and pockets. You don't have to finish the seams unless the fabric frays easily or you are going to wash the pants. Leave the pants unhemmed and the waistband unattached until the lining is inserted.

Sewing the lining Sew the lining together, including darts and pleats, and lengthen the zipper opening by 1 in. if the pants have a fly front zipper or by ½ in. for all other zippers. If you didn't raise the crotch curve when you cut the lining, raise the crotch curve by sewing with a ¼-in. seam allowance near the inseam that gradually blends to the ⅝-in. seamline at each end of the crotch curve. Stop sewing the crotch curve ½ in. to 1 in. below the zipper mark, back-stitch, then double-stitch the curve.

If you plan to connect the lining to the pants hem by machine, leave an 8-in. opening in one of the leg inseams a few inches below the crotch seam. This opening will allow you to reach between the layers to sew the hems.

Attaching the lining Before connecting the lining to the pants, press both thoroughly. Press the front darts toward the center front and the back darts toward the center back, then press the lining darts toward the side seams. Stitch down any lining pleats to keep them flat. Clean-finish the zipper area separately before inserting the lining (see pp. 86-88). Other-wise, slip the lining inside the pants and pin them together with wrong sides facing, matching centers, notches, and side seams.

Next, turn under the seam allowance at the zipper opening and attach the lining to the zipper by hand or by machine. Baste the lining and pants together at the waist seam using a ½-in. seam allowance. (If your pants have a fly front closure, the closure must be sewn before basting at the waist.)

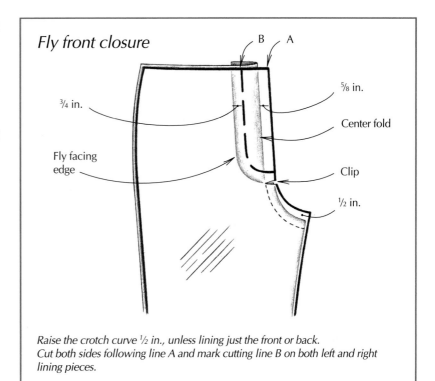

Fly front closure

B A

⁵⁄₈ in.

¾ in.

Center fold

Fly facing edge

Clip

½ in.

Raise the crotch curve ½ in., unless lining just the front or back. Cut both sides following line A and mark cutting line B on both left and right lining pieces.

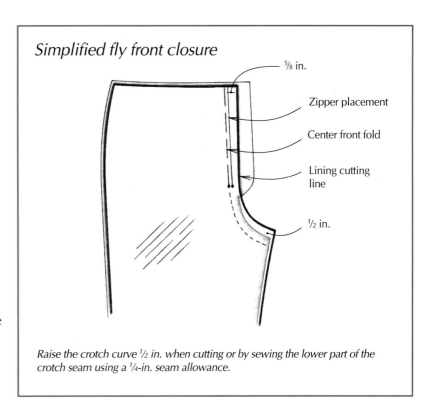

Simplified fly front closure

⁵⁄₈ in.

Zipper placement

Center front fold

Lining cutting line

½ in.

Raise the crotch curve ½ in. when cutting or by sewing the lower part of the crotch seam using a ¼-in. seam allowance.

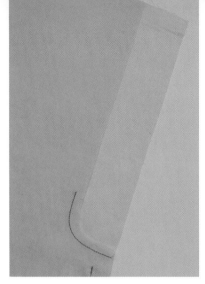

Stitch the lining together, then cut along the adjustment line after aligning to the pants with wrong sides facing. Staystitch along the lower curve using a ¼-in. seam allowance.

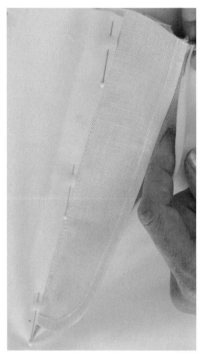

On the underlap, turn under and pin the seam allowance to connect the lining to the zipper tape or to the fly shield, then slipstitch or repin between the layers and machine-sew using a zipper foot.

If the lining is slightly smaller or firmer than the fashion fabric, sew with the lining on top. If the garment is firmer or slightly smaller at the waist seam, sew with the garment facing up so that the feed dogs on the machine distribute the excess ease evenly. With the zipper open, baste the waist seam from end to end, making sure the lining covers the zipper tape but is ⅛ in. to ¼ in. from the zipper teeth. The lining does not cover the zipper tape on the fly facing application. Next, install the waistband and hem the pants.

Connecting the lining to the fly front closure To attach the lining to the fly front closure, position the sewn lining inside the pants with wrong sides facing, then following the adjustment line, cut away the side of the lining that lines up to the fly facing. Staystitch the lower curve using a ¼-in. seam allowance, or if your pattern has a square fly facing instead of a curved one, staystitch and pivot at the inside corner. Clip the curve to the staystitching at ½-in. intervals, or clip to the corner if the bottom is square. Turn under a ⅜-in. seam allowance and slipstitch in place.

If you want to machine-sew the lining to the fly facing, pin the lining to the fly facing with right sides facing, aligning the raw edges, then use a zipper foot and a ⅜-in. seam allowance to sew in place.

On the underlap, turn under the seam allowance to connect to the zipper tape or to the fly shield, noting that the cut edges may not line up due to variations in the zipper placement. Then slipstitch or repin between the layers and machine-sew using a zipper foot.

Using a simplified fly front lining application The easy way to finish the lining edge at the zipper opening is by stitching a narrow machine-stitched hem just as is done on the standard zipper. If your fly opening has a fly shield, adjust the fly facing side of the lining so that it ends next to the edge of the fly shield when the zipper is closed.

To finish the lining at the fly closure without connecting to the zipper, sew the lining, leaving the lining zipper opening 1 in. longer than the garment zipper opening. Position the lining inside the pants with wrong sides facing, and adjust the fly facing side of the lining to clear the fly shield when the zipper is closed.

Using a pin or a marker, mark where the lining meets the edge of the fly shield along the waist seam, then add a ⅝-in. seam allowance and draw a line connecting to the original cutting line at the bottom of the zipper opening. Cut along the adjusted cutting line for the fly side only.

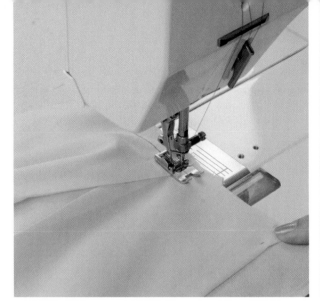

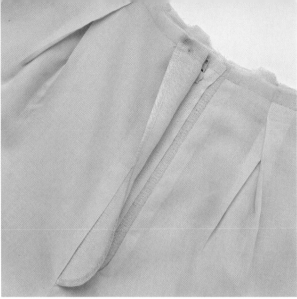

With the zipper open, machine-baste the waistline together with wrong sides facing.

After attaching the lining to the fly closure, machine-baste the waist seam and attach the waistband.

Next, press the zipper opening
⅝ in. to the wrong side from the
waist to the bottom of the zipper
opening, then turn and press the
raw edges to meet the foldline.
Stitching close to the second
fold, start sewing from the waist
down, pivot at the bottom of the
opening, sew across the bottom,
pivot, and sew the other side to
the waist. With the zipper open,
machine-baste the wrong side of
the lining to the wrong side of
the pants at the waist using a
½-in. seam allowance.

Free-hanging the lining hem
Finish the free-hanging lining
hem by pressing the bottom
edges under twice to make the
lining 1 in. shorter than the
pants' length and machine-
stitching close to the inner fold.
You can connect the lining

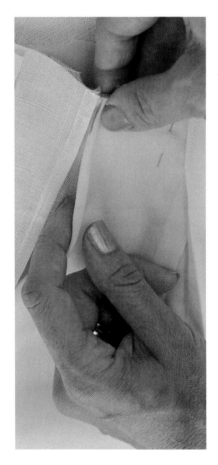

*To use the simplified lining
application, adjust the facing side of
the lining so that it ends next to the
edge of the fly shield when the
zipper is closed. Position the lining
inside the pants with wrong sides
facing and mark where the lining
meets the fly shield along the
waistline.*

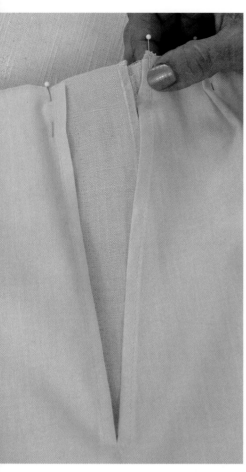

Press back the ⅝-in. seam allowance at the zipper opening, then turn back and press the raw edges to meet the foldline. Stitch both sides close to the inner fold using a continuous stitch and pivoting twice at the bottom of the zipper opening.

hem to the pants hem at the inseam and side seams using French tacks or quick tacks (see pp. 53-54), or you can leave the lining disconnected to press the pants more easily.

Connecting the lining hem to the pants If you want to connect the lining hem to the pants, sew the pants hem at least 1 in. below the raw edge. The lining length should be ⅝ in. longer than the finished pants length, so trim the lining if necessary. Turn back and pin the lining to the pants at the hem near the inseam, making sure the legs aren't twisted, then pull the leg through the inseam opening.

Remove the pin at the inseam and stuff the lining leg into the pants leg so you can align the raw edges with right sides facing. Pin and stitch the edges together using a ⅝-in. seam allowance, then pull the pants leg through to the right side and repeat for the other leg. Close the lining inseam by sewing the folded edges together using an edgestitch.

Partial pants lining

Partially lining the garment gives you the benefit of lining the area that is most visible, creases most easily, and has the most strain. On white or pastel-colored pants, be sure there is no differ-

ence between the lined and unlined area showing on the outside. If shading occurs, either fully line or underline the pants. (If underlining, see pp. 104-105.)

To partially line both the pants' front and back, follow the sewing directions for the full lining. Remember to cut the lining on the crossgrain using the selvage as the lower edge of each lining section. It is common to partially line just the pants' front or back, stopping below the knee area. Use this lining application to cover up the area with the most details or the greatest strain. The following describes partially lining the front when there is a fly opening.

Preparing the pants To prepare the pants, sew the darts and pleats, press, then sew in any slanted pockets. If there is a fly front, sew the crotch seam, stopping 2 in. below the zipper opening and leaving the lower section of the crotch seam unstitched, then install the zipper.

Sewing the lining Begin sewing the lining by sewing darts and pleats on each lining section and pressing in the opposite direction as the pants. Reinforce-stitch each lining section, starting at the zipper mark and ending 2 in. below. To sew the partial lining, baste each lining section to the corresponding pants section with wrong sides facing. Treat as one layer except when sewing darts, stitched-down pleats, and the zipper area. Cut away the side of the lining that lines up to the fly facing along the adjustment line, and staystitch the lower part of the curve using a ¼-in. seam allowance.

To finish the zipper area, line up and pin the wrong side of the lining to the wrong side of each pants front, starting with the crotch seam. Using a ½-in. seam allowance, machine-baste the lining to the unstitched lower part of each crotch seam, stopping at the stitching just below the zipper. Next, clip the lining seam allowance to the stay-stitching just below the fly shield if you have one or the fly facing. On the underlap side, press under the seam allowance to cover the zipper tape but clear the zipper teeth.

To attach the lining to the zipper, either slipstitch or sew between the layers by machine. The lining will not cover the zipper tape on the facing side. Clip the lining to the ¼-in. stay-stitching along the curve, then pin and sew the lining to the fly facing. To hand-sew, press back the ⅜-in. seam allowance and slipstitch to the fly facing. To

machine-sew, reach between the layers, lining up the edges with right sides facing, and sew using a ⅜-in. seam allowance and a zipper foot. Finally, serge, zigzag stitch, or pink the lower edge if you haven't already cut the lining so the selvage edge finishes the lower edge.

Attaching the lining To attach the lining to the garment, pin the wrong side of the lining to the wrong side of the pants front and baste the side seams, inseams, and waist. Now treating the pants and lining as one, sew the pants together.

Lining the knees You can also partially line the knee area in the front only to control stretching. To do this, serge, zigzag stitch, or pink the upper and lower edges of the lining sections, then pin each lining section to the appropriate leg section with wrong sides facing. Baste the side seams and inseams using a ½-in. seam allowance, and sew the pants as usual.

Underlining the pants

Using an underlining does not preclude using a lining; you can do both. However, I prefer to use the following method on pants because the underlining serves as a lining and also clean-finishes the seams. The best application

Turn back and pin the lining hem to the pants hem at the inseam, making sure the legs aren't twisted. Pull the leg through the lining opening, then pin and sew the hems together with right sides facing.

To adjust the underlining for turn of cloth, align each pants section and underlining section with right sides facing. Pin or baste, then fold along the center crease line with the fashion fabric around the underlining and trim the excess underlining along the vertical seams.

1-in. seam allowance that will become a ⅞-in. or ¾-in. allowance by the time you attach the underlining.

It is important to adjust the width of each lining section to allow for turn of cloth because the underlining is handled together with the fashion fabric as it curves around the body. To do this, position each underlining section on top of the corresponding pants section with right sides facing. Pin or baste along the center crease line, then fold the pants sections along the crease line with the fashion fabric around the underlining. This causes the underlining to extend past the fabric edges along the vertical seams. Trim any excess underlining; the thicker the fashion fabric, the more the underlining will have to be trimmed.

You can sew darts and stitched-down pleats on the pants layer and on the underlining layer individually, then attach the underlining, or you can attach the underlining, then sew the darts and stitched-down pleats after turning the pants section right side out.

for this technique is on fabrics that are loosely woven, transparent, or wrinkle-prone.

Adjusting the underlining for turn of cloth Begin preparing the underlining by cutting it the same as the fashion fabric. Next, you can either mark and sew darts and stitched-down pleats on the wrong side of the pants layer and on the wrong side of the underlining layer separately, or mark the darts and pleats on the right side of the underlining only if you are going to treat the underlining and pants layers as one (see pp. 83-85).

If you are sewing a lapped zipper, increase the seam allowance in the zipper area by ⅜ in. By doing this, you will be starting with a

Attaching the underlining To clean-finish the vertical seams, pin corresponding sections of the underlining and pants with right sides facing. Keeping the edges

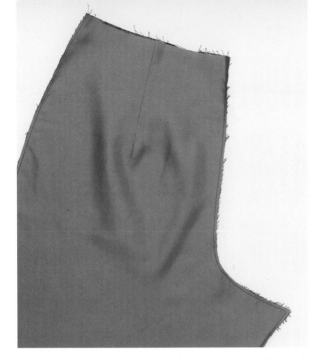

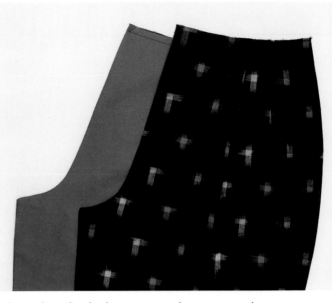

To clean-finish vertical seams, sew with right sides facing, using a ⅛-in. to ¼-in. seam allowance.

These clean-finished sections can be sewn together with the pants and underlining treated as one layer.

facing, sew the layers using a ⅛-in. seam allowance or, if the fashion fabric is thick or frays easily, a ¼-in. seam allowance. Don't sew the waist or hem yet. Next, clip the crotch curve and the corner point. Press seams open or toward the lining, turn right side out, then press seams along the edge.

Sewing the pants From this point on, treat the fashion fabric and underlining as one. Baste along the waist edge at ½ in. and through the center of each dart and pleat, going 1 in. past the end marks. Next, sew the darts and pleats if you haven't already sewn them separately. Continue in the usual sewing sequence, then sew the finished seams using a seam allowance of ½ in. or ⅜ in. if you attached the underlining using a ¼-in. seam allowance.

Hemming the pants To hem the pants, baste the fashion fabric and underlining along the hemline and fold back the hem. Adjust the hem allowance for turn of cloth, and trim away any underlining that may show past the hem edge. Finish the hem edge using seam binding or your favorite method.

7 Dress Linings

A lined dress slides easily over the body and has a smooth silhouette. The same fabrics that are appropriate for lining skirts are also good for lining dresses. Select rayon or polyester sheath lining, China silk, cotton or poly-cotton batiste or broadcloth, blouseweight microfiber, georgette, taffeta, silk or polyester crepe de Chine, charmeuse, and jacquards. As usual, the lining and fashion fabric must be compatible in regard to care requirements.

I prefer lining fabrics that do not wrinkle, which include polyester sheath lining, lightweight microfiber and polyester crepe de Chine, charmeuse, georgette, taffeta, and jacquards. Rayon fabrics typically wrinkle easily but it is worth checking each fabric you are considering because the fabric's weave affects the amount of wrinkling. Crush the sample in your palm to see how easily it releases wrinkles—you may have a pleasant surprise.

In this chapter, I will show you how to make a dress lining pattern, whether you will be using the classic or quick lining method. I'll then discuss the construction of many variations of dress linings, including full, partial, sleeveless dress, and strapless dress linings.

Making a Dress Lining Pattern

Making a lining pattern for a dress is very easy, whether you choose to use the classic or quick lining method or to line to the edge. To use the classic lining method, cut the dress lining using the main dress pattern pieces, excluding facings, inseam pockets, and overlays. Since dress facings often have acute curved edges, using a 3/8-in. seam allowance instead of the standard 5/8-in. seam allowance makes it easier to connect the lining to the facings when using the classic lining application.

To create a classic lining pattern, place the front and back neck facings under the front and back patterns, and mark the lining cutting line 3/4 in. from the inner facing edge. Adjust the lining cutting length to equal the finished length of the dress plus 5/8 in. (see the illustration below.)

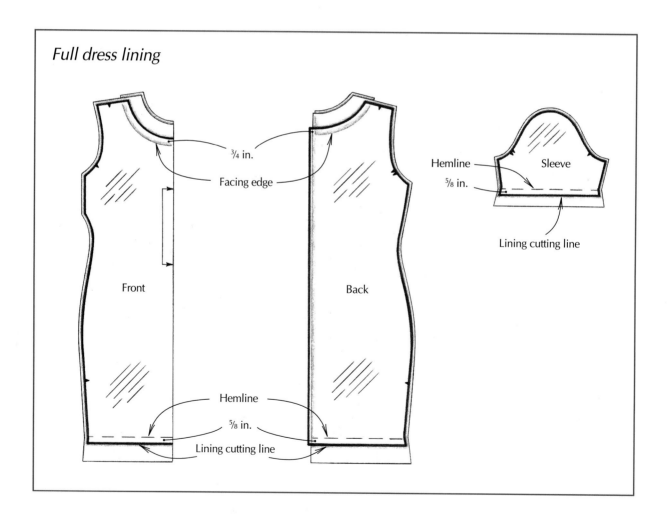

Full dress lining

3/4 in.

Facing edge

Front

Back

Hemline

5/8 in.

Lining cutting line

Hemline

5/8 in.

Sleeve

Lining cutting line

If the dress style has shoulder pads thicker than ¼ in., lower the slope of the front and back shoulder seam at the armhole by one-half the thickness of the shoulder pad and connect to the original line near the neck. Also lower the sleeve cap by the full thickness of the shoulder pad, blending to the original cutting line at the notches. Raise the underarm seam on dresses with sleeves when you set in the sleeve by using a ¼-in. seam allowance at the underarm that blends to the ⅝-in. seam at the notches.

The quick lining looks the same as the classic but is faster and easier to construct. To cut the lining pattern, simply use the main dress pattern pieces for the sections that you want to line. The facing pieces will be sewn directly onto the lining pieces, thus eliminating the need to interface the facings.

When the fashion fabric is bulky or scratchy, you can eliminate the facings and line the dress to the edge. In this case, also use the main dress pattern pieces to cut the lining.

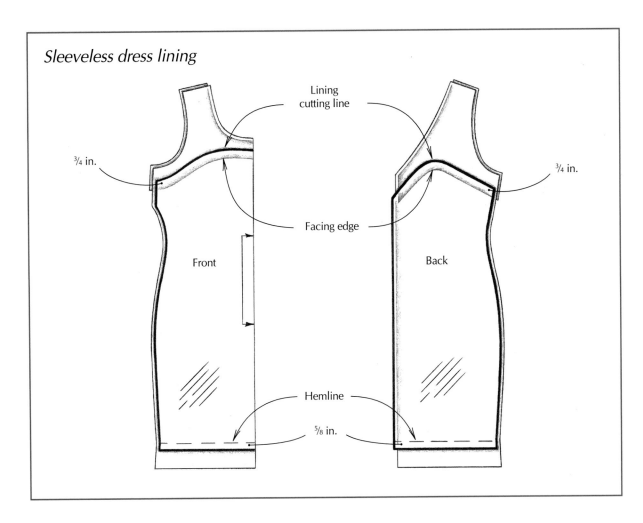

Sleeveless dress lining

Lining cutting line

¾ in.

¾ in.

Facing edge

Front

Back

Hemline

⅝ in.

Sleeveless dresses and jumpers often have combined neck and armhole facings. To create the lining pattern, position each facing beneath the corresponding dress pattern and mark the lining cutting line ¾ in. beyond the facing edge (see the illustration on p. 109). Then mark the cutting line ⅝ in. below the finished hemline. You also have the option of using the quick lining method or lining to the edge.

Constructing and Inserting a Dress Lining

Construction techniques differ depending on what kind of lining you want to use in your dress. Following are instructions for full and partial linings, as well as methods for lining sleeveless dresses or jumpers.

Full dress lining using the classic or quick method

The difference between the classic and quick lining methods lies in how the lining unit is cut and assembled. In the classic method, the garment pattern is adjusted to create the lining pattern, and the lining is attached to the interfaced facings with a conventional seam. With the quick lining method, there is no need to create a lining pattern; the lining is cut just like the dress and the

facings are stitched on top of the lining. Another benefit of the quick lining is that you don't have to interface the neck facings because the lining runs underneath the facings and helps to stabilize the neckline.

Preparing the dress Sew the dress together, including sleeves and pockets, and insert the zipper. Next, stitch the hem of the dress.

Sewing the classic lining unit Interface the front and back neck facings using fusible interfacing, then sew the shoulder seams with right sides facing. Trim the shoulder seam allowances to ¼ in. and press the seams open. Sew the lining together, including setting in the sleeves. Next, staystitch the neckline using a ¼-in. seam allowance and clip to the stitching line at ½-in. intervals. Pin and sew the lining to the unnotched facing edge using a ⅜-in. seam allowance and press the facing seam toward the lining. Finally, press the lining seams open, the armhole seams toward the sleeves, and the darts and pleats in the opposite direction of the dress darts and pleats.

Sewing the quick lining unit Sew the front neck facing to the back neck facing at the shoulders, trim the seams to ¼ in. and press open, then press under but don't sew the unnotched edge. It is much

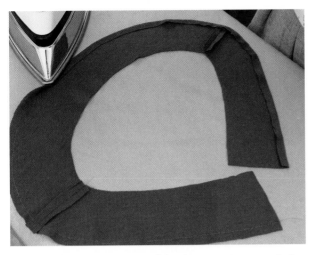

Staystitch the outer curve of the facing using staystitch plus at the sharp curves near the shoulder seam, then press the seam allowance back along the stitching line.

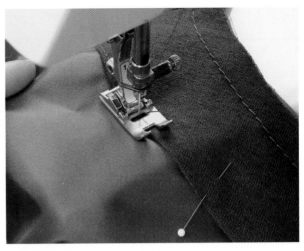

Attach the wrong side of the facing to the right side of the lining, aligning the neck seam. Baste the neck seam and edgestitch the facing's folded edge to the lining.

easier to press back a curved edge if you staystitch ¼ in. from the raw edge and press back along the stitching line. Remember to use staystitch plus along off-grain edges and outside curves (see the sidebar on p. 90).

Next, sew the front and back lining at the shoulders and press the seams open, then place the wrong side of the facing on top of the right side of the lining, aligning the edges. Machine-baste the raw edges together using a ½-in. seam allowance, and edgestitch the folded edge to the lining using the standard stitch length. Finish sewing the lining by stitching the side seams and attaching the sleeves. Press the lining seams open, the armhole seams toward the sleeves, and the darts and pleats in the opposite direction of the dress darts and pleats.

Attach the lining and facings to the dress as a unit by pinning and sewing the neck seam with right sides facing.

Inserting the facing/lining unit

After the lining is sewn, attach the lining and facings as a unit to the dress by pinning along the neck seam with right sides facing and stitching. Grade and clip the neck seam, then press the seam allowances toward the lining and understitch. Finish the zipper area using one of the methods on pp. 86-88.

Press back the lining hem to be the same length as the finished dress length. Trim the lining hem allowance if it is more than ⅝ in., then slipstitch to the upper part of the dress hem.

To finish the sleeves, sew the dress sleeve hem, then press up the lining sleeve hem and slipstitch in place. If you prefer, you can connect the lining sleeve hem to the dress sleeve hem by machine, following the directions on pp. 37-39.

To finish the hem, you may choose to install a free-hanging lining hem, which is suitable for all types of dress silhouettes. To do this, press up and sew the dress hem, then press up and machine-sew the lining hem separately so that it is 1 in. shorter than the dress.

If the dress you are sewing has a straight silhouette, you also have the option of connecting the lining hem to the dress hem. First, press the lining hem to be the same length as the finished dress length, then pin the folded edge to just cover the raw edges of the dress hem and slipstitch.

Full dress lining to the edge

If you want to line a dress to the edge, cut the lining the same as the dress and attach it to the dress at the neck seam following the directions for inserting the facing/lining unit. This method requires the neck to be interfaced (the interfacing should be cut using the facing pattern). Use fusible interfacing to interface either the dress neckline or the lining neckline.

Partial dress lining

There are different ways to partially line a dress depending on the style. Partial linings are efficient because only the areas that benefit the most are lined while the dress is kept lightweight.

Eliminating the sleeve lining If you like to push up your sleeves as I do, then eliminate the sleeve lining and line just the body of the dress. To do this, construct the dress, including setting in the sleeves, then construct the lining minus the sleeves and attach it to the dress following the directions for inserting the facing/lining unit. Machine-baste the lining armhole to the dress armhole, then bind the armhole using a bias binding cut from the lining fabric (see the sidebar on the facing page).

HOW TO BIND THE ARMHOLE

To bind the armhole, cut two bindings on the true bias from the lining fabric that measure 3 in. wide and 2 in. longer than the length of the armhole. Fold the binding in half lengthwise with wrong sides facing, and press a soft fold.

Pin the binding to the armhole edge of the garment, starting at the underarm, then unpin to sew the ends, adjusting the seam allowance to fit the armhole. Trim the seam allowance to ¼ in. and press the seam open, then stitch the armscye using a ⅝-in. seam allowance. Trim to ⅜ in. and press the seam allowances flat. Turn the binding over and around the seam and sew in place using an edgestitch, narrow zigzag stitch, or slipstitch.

You can also bind the armhole using a Hong Kong finish or bias tricot trim. These create a less bulky binding because you use a single layer of fabric to wrap around the seam.

Sew the binding ends, adjusting the seam allowance to fit the armhole, then trim the seam allowance to ¼ in. and press open. After sewing the binding to the armscye, trim the seam allowance to ⅜ in.

Another option is to overlock the armhole seam, attaching the lining to the dress and sleeve seam. You may also overlock the lining armhole separately just to finish the edge, then hand- or machine-tack the lining to the dress at the underarm seam. This is good to do when the outside fabric has quite a bit of give.

Extending the dress lining to below the seat To derive the benefits of lining the body of the dress, cut the lining pattern so it ends at the area below the seat.

Lining the bodice Dresses with a waist seam can be lined above the waist only. This method, which lines the area with the most details while the skirt remains unlined, is appropriate for dresses and jumpers with full skirts. To finish the waist seam, press the seam allowances toward the bodice, then press under the lining seam allowance and slipstitch to the waist seam.

Sleeveless dress lining

Following is my favorite way to line and sew a sleeveless dress without or with a center back opening because all the seams, including the armholes and shoulders, are stitched on the sewing machine. This method can also be used for sleeveless tops or jumpers.

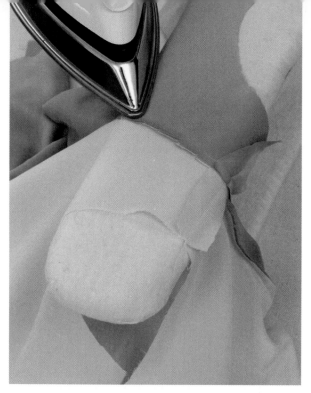

At the neckline, press the seam allowance toward the lining, or press open for a reversible garment.

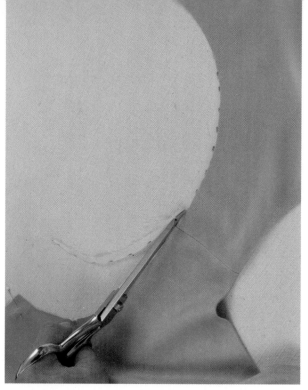

Trim the lining layer to be the same width as the garment at the shoulder seams.

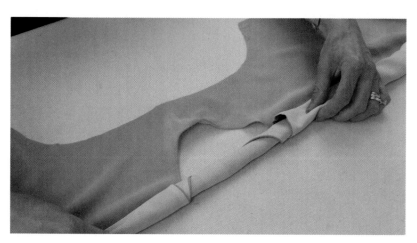

Roll the garment toward the armhole you will be sewing, stopping when the garment is next to the armscye.

Dresses without a center back opening For this version, the dress is lined to the edge and hemmed separately. The following directions also apply when sewing a reversible or lined top connected at the hem. Begin

by cutting the lining using the same pattern as the main garment pieces. Sew the front garment piece to the back at the shoulder seams and do the same with the lining pieces.

After pressing the seams open, pin and sew the garment neckline to the lining neckline. Trim or grade and clip the seams, then press the seam allowance toward the lining and under-stitch the neck seam. If the garment is reversible, press the neck seam open. Turn the garment right side out and press the neck seam flat along the edge.

Pin all four armhole ends to the corresponding lining. If the garment is not reversible, trim the lining to be the same width as the garment at the shoulder seams because understitching the neckline causes the lining to roll out past the shoulder edge. Don't trim the underarm area as this part of the lining is not affected. If you are making a reversible garment, there is no need to trim the lining layer.

The next step is to sew an enclosed seam at each armhole. Begin by rolling the garment toward the armhole you will be sewing, stopping when the garment is next to the armscye. Pin and sew the garment and lining armscye with right sides facing and the rolled garment in between, then trim or grade and clip the seam allowance. Press the seam toward the lining. For a reversible garment, press the seam open. Pull the garment right side out through the shoulder, then top-press the armhole so the seam is centered along the edge. Repeat these steps to sew the other armhole.

Using a continuous seam, sew one side of the garment front to the garment back and one side of the lining front to the lining back, being sure to match the underarm seams with right sides facing. Repeat for the other side, leaving a 6-in. opening along the lining side seams only if you are sewing a lined top and plan to connect the lower edges. Press the side seams open, and clip the lining side seams near the underarm if necessary to help

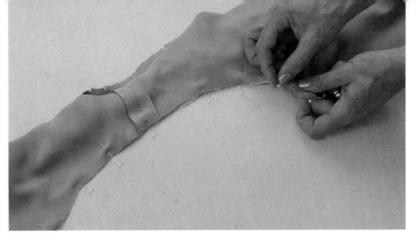

Pin and sew the garment and lining armscye with right sides facing.

them lie flat. Hem the dress and lining separately, sewing the lining hem to be 1 in. shorter than the finished dress length.

Tops can be hemmed separately or together with the lining layer or reversible layer. To hem tops separately, both layers can be hemmed the same length since the inside layer can be worn tucked into the skirt or pants when you wear the top out.

When sewing a reversible or lined top, you can easily connect the lower edge of the lining to the lower edge of the top by machine just as is done in ready-to-wear. After sewing and pressing the side seams open, leave the top and the lining wrong sides out. Lay the attached lining on top of the top. Match and pin the lower edges of the top to the lower edges of the lining with right sides facing, working all the way around the bottom edge.

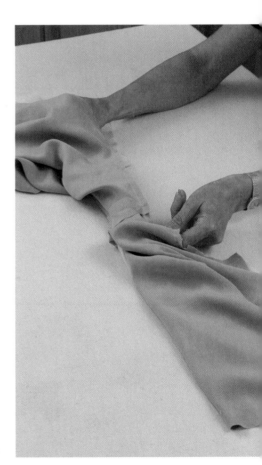

Pull the garment right side out through the shoulder seam.

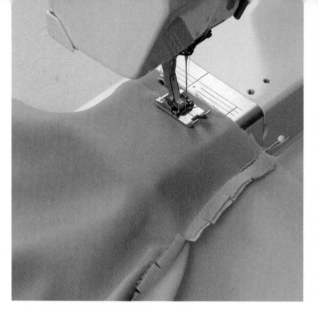

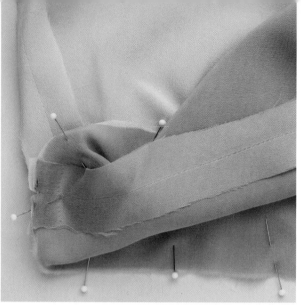

Sew the side seams with right sides facing, being sure to line up the underarm seams.

After pressing the side seams open, leave the top and lining with wrong sides out. Lay the attached lining on top of the top, match and pin the lower edge of the top to the lower edge of the lining with right sides facing, and stitch in a continuous circle.

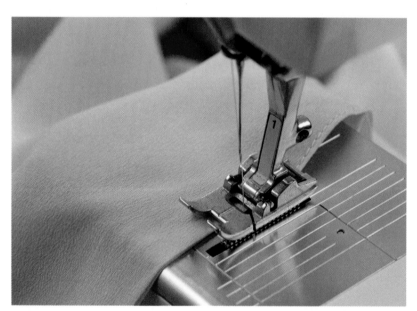

After pressing the seams open and turning the garment right side out, close the opening using an edgestitch.

Stitch in a continuous circle, leaving an opening along the lower edge for a reversible top. If you are making a lined top, you already left an opening along the lining side seam. Press the seam open and turn right side out through the lower opening or the lining opening. To close the opening at the lower edge, use a small piece of fusible web or edgestitch the entire hem. You may also close the lining side seam opening by edgestitching.

Dresses with a center back opening For this version, you can eliminate the facings if the fashion fabric is thick or scratchy. Otherwise, if you are keeping the facings, you can use the classic method to cut and sew the lining to the facings or the quick method to sew the

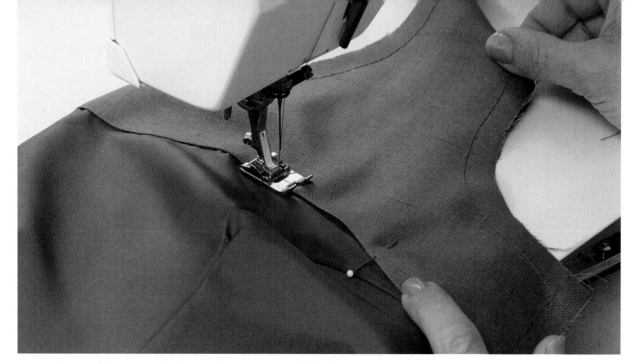

To use the quick lining method, sew the wrong side of the facing on top of the right side of the lining.

facings on top of the lining. The following directions describe sewing the lining using the quick lining method, but the sewing sequence for attaching the lining unit to the dress remains the same for all methods.

Begin by cutting the lining the same as the dress. Press under ¼ in. on the lower edges of the front and back facings. Next, pin the wrong sides of the facings to the right sides of the lining. Edgestitch the lower edge of the facings to the lining, then machine-baste the other facing edges to the lining ½ in. from the edges.

Sew the dress front to the dress back at the shoulders and press seams open, then sew the front lining/facing unit to the back

lining/facing unit at the shoulders and press seams open. Trim the lining/facing shoulder seams to ¼ in. After matching the lining to the dress at the neck and armholes with right sides facing, stitch the neck seam, stopping 1¼ in. from the back edge to allow for the zipper application. Sew both armholes, then trim or grade the seams and clip them. Press the seams flat, then press the seam allowances toward the lining.

Turn the dress to the right side by pulling it through the front shoulders, and top-press the seams. Next, sew the center back seam of the dress, insert the zipper, and sew the center back seam of the lining. Finish sewing the lining/facing unit to the neck seam above the zipper opening

When lining sleeveless garments, make the lining layer slightly narrower than the fashion fabric near the shoulder if the fashion fabric is medium-weight to thick. Trim the lining or lining/facing unit ⅛ in. narrower than the garment at the shoulder and blend to the original line near the under-arm. Doing this keeps the facings and lining from rolling out at the armhole.

Sew the dress at the shoulder seams, then sew the facing/lining unit at the shoulder seams and press seams open.

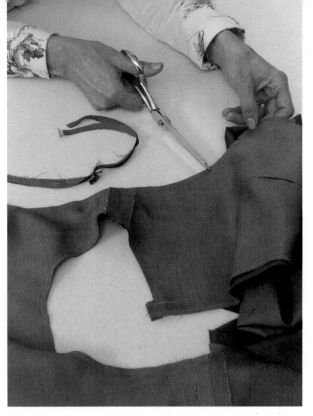

Stitch the neck seam, starting and stopping 1¼ in. from the back edge to allow for the zipper application and sew both armholes. Then trim or grade seams and clip curves.

Turn the dress right side out by reaching through the shoulders and pulling the back through to the outside.

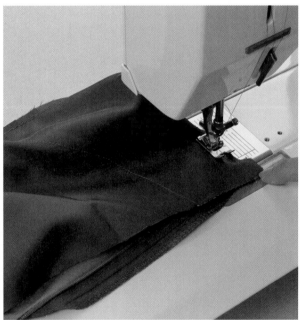

Finish sewing the lining/facing unit to the neck seam above the zipper with right sides facing.

and understitch the neckline, starting and stopping as close as possible to the shoulder seams.

With underarm seams matching, sew the lining front to the lining back and the dress front to the dress back with right sides facing and using a continuous stitch. Press the side seams open, clipping the side seams near the armscye if necessary, then understitch each armhole, starting as close as possible to the shoulder seam, continuing around the side seam, and stopping as close as possible to the other side of the shoulder seam. Machine-tack or hand-tack the facing side seam to the dress side seam at the underarm to hold in place. Hem the garment and lining separately.

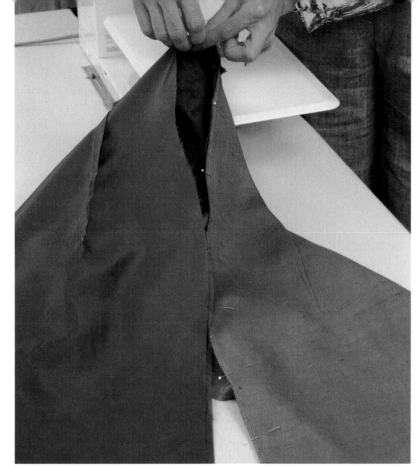

Pin and sew the side seams, being sure to match the underarm seams. Sew the lining front and back with right sides facing and the dress front and back with right sides facing with a continuous seam.

LINING STRAPLESS DRESSES

Strapless dress patterns often have a foundation layer made from the lining fabric in addition to the lining. It is also common for the lining of a strapless dress to serve as the foundation layer. In both situations, the lining fabric plays a major supporting role.

Close-fitting and usually in need of boning, strapless dresses and off-the-shoulder styles need a crisp, tightly woven, firm lining that is not slippery. If the fashion fabric you are using is taffeta, silk-faced satin, peau de soie, cotton, or a polyester satin with a dull finish, use the same fabric to line the bodice to create a luxurious and firm foundation for the dress. When self-lining is not possible because the fashion fabric is too thick, soft, or scratchy, I like to use polyester taffeta, which is available in a plain or moiré finish, to line the bodice.

Because you need strong support for a strapless or off-the-shoulder style, there are some lining fabrics that do not work. Most polyester and acetate satins have a slippery finish that makes it difficult to prevent the dress from sliding downward no matter how tightly you shape the seams. Acetate linings are poor candidates for tight bodices because they can't take any stress and fray easily at darts and seams. Although soft linings are not appropriate for lining the bodice area, you can use them for the rest of the dress.

8 Lace and Sheer Garment Linings

The fabric you select to line lace and sheer garments becomes an integral part of the total design. Because the lining will be visible, its color is important. You can use the lining color to modify the tone of a sheer fabric, and you can also get an interesting, sometimes iridescent effect by layering sheer fabrics of different colors.

The decision to use a sheer or opaque lining greatly influences the final design. Sheer and semisheer linings keep the garment light and airy, while opaque linings result in a more solid, structured style. Sheer tunics and skirts lined with one or more layers of sheer fabric result in diaphanous, filmy garments.

For best results, the drape of the lining fabric should be similar to that of the fashion fabric, but there are exceptions. For example, you can use a crisp net to fill out a gathered skirt made from a soft lace or silk chiffon. Similar drape in the lining and fashion fabric is most important when the lining is connected to all of the garment edges, such as on a jacket where you can't add a back pleat or a jump hem. You should line dresses, tunics, camisoles, and pants with the lining hemmed separately from the garment.

In this chapter, I will recommend some lining fabrics for lace and sheer garments and tell you how to make a lining pattern. I'll then show you how to insert a lining, including how to finish the garment's edges.

Choosing Lining Fabrics

For lace garments, silk, rayon, or polyester chiffon, silk or polyester organza, and cotton lawn, gauze, or organdy make good sheer lining fabrics. English net or tulle can be used for underlining. Silk, rayon, or polyester georgette is semisheer and makes a nice lining because its texture is slightly elastic, as is the net background of the lace fabric. Suitable opaque lining fabrics include satin, peau de soie, taffeta, crepe de Chine, charmeuse, faille, rayon or polyester sheath lining, and China silk.

The color of the lace fabric can be changed dramatically by the color of the lining. When choosing a color, the closest match between the lining and lace fabric is usually the poorest choice because you lose the interesting lace design. You should place linings that are close to but not the same shade as the lace color under the lace fabric to see which brings out the design without changing the lace's overall color.

Contrasting-colored linings emphasize the lace pattern with dramatic or delicate results, such as when combining a hot-pink lining with black lace or a peach lining with white lace. When you select a multicolored lace, you can use the lining color to emphasize different colors in the lace design and to change the mood of the fabric. By using one of the lace colors as the lining color, you de-emphasize that color in the lace design and bring out the others. Another possibility for both lace and sheer garments is to use a flesh-tone lining.

For sheer garments, I prefer to use luxurious opaque lining fabrics. These include silk, rayon, or polyester crepe de Chine, charmeuse, and faille. Georgette is nice under chiffon because it has a similar drape and the matte finish gives the illusion of using many chiffon layers together. If you need a crisp lining, try peau de soie or taffeta. Jacquards, printed fabrics, and moiré taffetas are interesting if the garment style is simple. Rayon and polyester sheath linings and China silk are also appropriate but are not as luxurious.

Making a Lining Pattern

When making a lace or sheer garment, you have the option of using an attached lining or a separate one. If you are making an attached lining, eliminate the facings and use the main pattern pieces to cut your lining, then line the garment completely to the edge. If you decide to connect the lining to follow the contour of a scalloped lace edge, increase the seam allowance by the depth of the scallop so that the lining will extend ⅝ in. beyond the outer scalloped edge. There is no need to increase the seam allowance to connect the lining to the scalloped edge in a straight line. If you are sewing a lining that is not connected to the garment, you can modify the main pattern pieces to create a lining pattern or even choose a completely different pattern.

Sewing a separate lining that is worn under the garment is a versatile way to line sheer and lace garments. By changing the lining, which can be a dress, camisole, or half-slip, you change the mood of the outfit. You can also use different necklines and silhouettes to play up the sheer outer garment. For example, you can line a high-neck, long-sleeve tunic or dress with a camisole or slip that has a sleeveless scoop neck or spaghetti straps. Or you can line a full or gathered dress with a narrower and shorter lining to turn the garment's silhouette into a halo of sheer color.

Inserting a Lining and Finishing Edges

You can adapt almost any pattern for sewing a lined lace garment by eliminating the shaped facings and interfacing and bringing the lining to the edge.

Lace garments

To assemble a lace garment and lining, follow the sewing sequence in the appropriate chapter for the style garment you are making. If your lace is not very sheer, you should be able to attach the lining to the garment with right sides facing as on conventional garments. If the lace is very sheer, match the wrong side of the lining to the right side of the garment to insert the lining and finish the edges. By doing this, the seams won't show through the lace design when you turn the lining inside the garment and the right side of the lining faces out when you wear the garment.

After attaching the lining, sew a lace trim on top of the edges to cover the conventional seam. Hem the lining separately, making the lining 1 in. shorter than the garment. The lining on lace jackets is usually connected at the hem. You may connect the lining in a straight line or by following the scalloped edge. You can also sew allover lace fabrics following the directions on pp. 125-127. In that case, use French bindings or bias facings to finish the edges instead of using lace trim.

Adding a scalloped trim to finish the edge The scalloped edge of the lace is an attractive way to finish the edge of the garment. You may cut the lace trim from the lace fabric's outer

To line lace skirts and pants with waistbands so the right side of the lining faces out, just baste the right side of the lining to the wrong side of the garment at the waistline, then add the waistband.

edge or you can purchase a separate trim. To finish the neckline or armscye with a scalloped edge, pin the wrong side of the lace trim to the right side of the garment so that the innermost points of the scallop line up with the finished garment edge. Be sure to center the scalloped edge at the center front and at other prominent areas. On most laces, there is no need to turn back the ends at the back opening; simply cut away the excess trim following the edge of the lace motif.

If you are applying the scalloped edge to an armhole or any other continuous edge, place the seam in the least conspicuous place, such as at the underarm or side seam. Overlap the lace edge and cut away the excess lace following the lace contour.

Following the lace edge, sew in place by hand using a slipstitch or by machine using a straight or zigzag stitch. If you are machine-sewing, use a thread that blends with the lace you are using, such as fine silk thread or rayon machine-embroidery thread for laces that shine. On cotton laces, use fine machine-embroidery cotton thread. If the lace is heavy and you are sewing through a thick layer, you may need to use all-purpose polyester thread. If you are hand-sewing, you can use the same thread for the edge as you did for the rest of the garment since a hand-sewn stitch is less prominent.

Connecting the lining to a scalloped edge If you are connecting the lining or under-lining to a scalloped-edge lace, the fabric edge can be finished with a straight line following the innermost point in the scallop or with a curved line following the shape of the scallop. To use a straight line, pin or baste the lining near the scalloped edge and cut the lining ¼ in. longer than the scallop's innermost point. Turn under the lining edge and slipstitch to the lace.

To follow the curve of the lace, pin the lining near the scalloped edge and trace the outline of the scallop onto the lining using white dressmaker carbon. Staystitch along the marked line, pivoting at points, and trim, leaving a ¼-in. seam allowance. Reposition the lining and

To finish the neckline or armscye with a scalloped edge, pin the lace scallop on top of the garment so the innermost edge of each scallop lines up to the finished edge of the garment. Overlap the lace edge and cut away the excess lace following the lace contour.

Following the lace edge, machine-sew the lace in place using a narrow zigzag stitch or hand-sew using a slipstitch.

Turn under the lining edge and slipstitch in place. Depending on the density and complexity of the lace pattern, you may be able to use a zigzag stitch in place of hand-sewing.

scallops and baste to hold in place. Fold the lining back along the stitching line, clip the corners, and slipstitch to the scalloped edge.

Sheer garments

Attaching the lining to sheer garments is different than attaching to conventional opaque garments. On sheer garments, the right side of the lining faces the wrong side of the garment so that the lining seams will not show. Since the lining seams are exposed on the wrong side of the garment, you should use French seams to sew the lining or use seam finishes.

Assemble the garment, but don't install the zipper if there is one until you've attached the lining. Cut the lining the same as the garment, then sew the lining together. If the garment has a zipper, see p. 85 on sewing the zipper seam. Treat the garment

UNDERLINING LACE GARMENTS

It is not unusual for a commercial pattern designed with lace in mind to recommend underlining the lace to better support the garment's silhouette. Pattern directions often specify using organza as the underlining fabric.

Organza makes a fine under-lining for firm laces such as alençon or crisp metallic or polyester laces. However, it is too rigid for those with high rayon contents, such as most Chantilly and Venise laces, also called Guipure laces, which tend to be soft and drapey. If you want to underline a soft lace, try using tulle, a sheer tricot such as one used in lingerie, or stretch illusion.

You can test to see if the lace has a tendency to droop by connecting it to the underlining before you cut anything. Working on a flat surface, place the underlining fabric under the lace and baste together a rectangular area about 12 in. wide and 18 in. long. Leave the basted area in a vertical position for about 24 hours by pinning the upper edge to a dress form or an upright ironing board. Soft laces will pull away from the underlining layer and have excess length near the lower basting line.

If there is a problem, try another underlining fabric or cut tricot crosswise so that the stretch follows the lengthwise direction of the fabric. The other option is to separate the lace from the underlining near the hem. Heavy and open laces are rarely connected to the lining or underlining hem in ready-to-wear. Instead, they are caught in the shoulder, neck seam, and armhole and left unattached at the bottom.

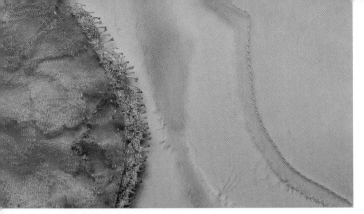

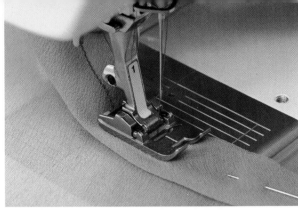

Outline the scalloped edge onto the lining, staystitch along the marked line, and trim the seam allowance to ¼ in. Fold the lining back along the staystitching, clip corners, and slipstitch invisibly in place following the scalloped edge.

When using French binding, pin the binding to the right side of the garment so that it conforms to the garment edge and sew in place.

You can also use French bindings or bias facings to finish just the garment neckline when you use a detached lining.

layer and the lining layer as one at the zipper opening to prevent the zipper from showing through to the outside.

After sewing the lining together, baste it to the wrong side of the garment at the neckline and openings. Treating the garment and lining as a single layer, finish the edges using French bindings or bias facings. Hem the garment using a narrow machine-stitched or hand-stitched hem or a rolled hem. The lining should be hemmed separately to be 1 in. shorter than the garment.

Finishing edges with a French or double binding An attractive finish for necklines and armholes on sheer garments is using a French binding, also called a double binding. To do this, staystitch the edge of the garment just beyond the seam-line to prevent stretching, then trim away the seam allowance. Next, cut a bias strip six times the desired width plus ¼ in. to ⅜ in. to allow for stretching and

turning. For example, you will cut the bias 1¾ in. wide for a ¼-in. binding. The length of the bias should be 2 in. longer than the garment edge. Once the bias is cut, fold the strip in half lengthwise, with wrong sides facing, and press lightly.

Pin the binding to the right side of the garment, aligning the raw edges and stretching the binding slightly on the inside curves. Stitch a ¼-in. seam, press the seam toward the binding, then trim the excess binding at the neckline or sleeve opening to ½ in. Next, turn in the ends of the binding, fold the binding in half over the raw edges, and pin. Slipstitch the folded edge of the binding to the previous stitching line and press. If you want to sew the last step by machine, fold the binding around the seam allowance, being sure the folded edge covers the neck seam, then pin on the right side and stitch on the binding and next to the seam or stitch in the well of the seam.

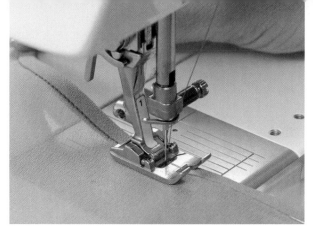

To finish by machine, stitch on the binding and next to the seam or sew in the well of the seam.

Press the binding toward the neckline.

When sewing the binding to a circular or continuous edge, begin and end sewing the seam 3 in. from the ends. Trim the bias length so that the seam allowances measure the same width as the folded binding. If you are using a 1¾-in. binding, cut the seam allowances to ⅞ in. Unfold the binding, then fold the ends diagonally to form a square, and finger-press the seamline. The seam is on the straight of grain. Next, stitch the binding seam with right sides facing, matching the finger-pressed seamlines, then trim to ¼ in. and press open. Refold the binding and finish stitching the seam.

Using bias binding as a facing

Another edge-finishing method uses a narrow bias binding as a facing that is turned to the inside of the garment. The topstitching is all that will show on the outside of the garment.

If the garment seam allowance is ⅝ in., trim the garment to ¼ in. by staystitching ⅜ in. from the edge and trimming just next to the stitch. If the seam allowance is ¼ in., staystitch ¼ in. from the edge.

Next, cut the binding 1½ in. wide on the bias. Fold the strip in half with wrong sides facing, and press lightly. Pin the binding to the right side of the garment, aligning the edges, sew using a ¼-in. seam allowance and clip the seam if necessary. Press the binding toward the neckline and trim the excess at the opening to ½ in.

If you are sewing to a circular or continuous edge, curve the ends of the binding into the seam allowance at an inconspicuous place, such as just past the shoulder seam. Sew using a ¼-in. seam allowance and cut away the excess.

Fold the binding to the wrong side and press, then press back the binding ends. Topstitch from the right side close to the neckline edge of the binding.

9 Sweater Linings

Sweater jackets and coats benefit greatly from the addition of a lining because most sweater knits have nappy surface textures that cling easily to other fabrics and are often thick but not very wind resistant. The lining adds warmth and insulation and makes the garment slide easily over other clothes. To make a sweater easier to wear, choose lining fabrics such as rayon or polyester sheath lining, China silk, microfiber, silk or polyester crepe de Chine, charmeuse, and jacquards. Select the one that is most compatible in weight and maintenance with the sweater layer. To add warmth or an insulated layer, use a flannel-backed satin, a quilted fabric, or wool jersey, which is warm and elastic. Otherwise select a thin, tightly woven fabric such as microfiber to maximize the wind-breaking effect without adding thickness.

Sweater jackets and coats are easy to line because they have simple shapes. It is possible to line sweater knits with woven linings because these garments usually have ample ease. If you plan to line a close-fitting sweater that stretches as it fits over the body, then you must use a lining fabric that has the same degree of stretch as the sweater knit. Light- to medium-weight jersey, tricot, and interlock knits make good lining fabrics that stretch.

In this chapter, I will show you how to make a lining pattern for a sweater jacket or coat and how to sew, attach, and finish the lining.

To copy the sweater shape, outline the sweater on pattern paper, adding a ⅝-in. seam allowance except at the bottom ribbing.

Mark both the front and back necklines on the same pattern, adding a ⅝-in. seam allowance. First cut both layers of paper to the higher neckline, then unfold the paper and cut only half the pattern with the lower neckline.

Making a Sweater Lining Pattern

To make a lining pattern, you will outline the shape of the sweater jacket or coat onto some pattern paper. Begin by folding the paper and the garment at the center or by lining up the folded paper to the center of the sweater. With centers matched and the garment on top of the paper, copy the shape. To copy

the armhole, either lift the sleeve and mark the paper at the armhole seam or run a spoked tracing wheel over the armhole seam to leave indentation marks on the pattern.

Before marking the side seams, look at the side seams of the garment you are copying. With the exception of longer garments such as some tunics or sweater dresses, side seams are usually straight and follow a vertical rib. If the garment has a ribbed bottom, the bottom will probably have a curved-in shape, while the sleeve pulling across the chest causes that area to look wider when it is not. On the pattern, use a ruler to draw the side seams, using the width just below the sleeves to keep the width consistent all the way to the bottom of the ribbing.

Next, mark the neck seam, which is where you will connect the lining to the sweater, by lifting the neck trim or by using the tracing wheel. If the sweater has ribbing, do not include the width of the ribbing when marking. Mark both the front and back necklines on the same pattern.

Use a ruler and French curve to true the lines, then add a ⅝-in. seam allowance and cut both pattern layers on that line. Cut both pattern layers along the higher or back neckline, then unfold the pattern and cut half the pattern using the lower or front neckline, being sure to add a ⅝-in. seam allowance. Stop cutting at the front fold.

To copy the sleeve, place the sleeve fold on the paper fold and outline. True the lines, add a ⅝-in. seam allowance, and cut through both pattern layers so you'll have a full sleeve pattern when the pattern is open.

Once the pattern is completed, cut the lining, adding a 1-in. seam allowance at the front opening and a 1-in. pleat at the center back (see the illustration below). The length should be cut equal to the length of the sweater plus a 1-in. hem allowance. If you are lining a full-length sweater, cut the lining

2 in. longer than the finished garment to allow for differences in fabric. Cut the sleeve lining the same length as the sleeve plus a 1-in. hem allowance.

Constructing and Inserting a Sweater Lining

Sweater linings are fast and easy to sew because sweaters have simple shapes.

Sewing the lining

Sew the lining pieces together by using conventional seams and pressing the seams open or by using a serger. Seam finishes are

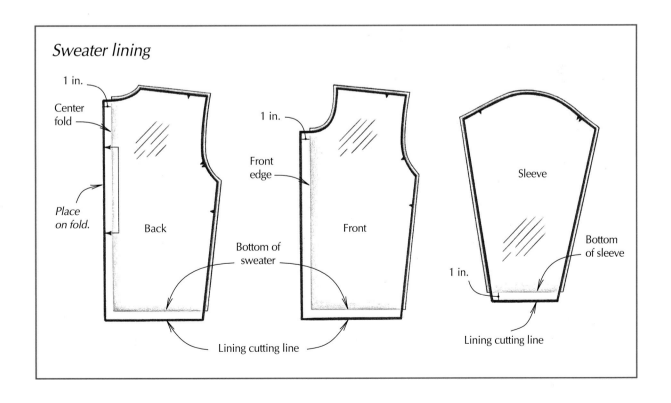

Sweater lining

1 in.
Center fold
Place on fold.
Back
Bottom of sweater
Lining cutting line

1 in.
Front edge
Front
Lining cutting line

Sleeve
Bottom of sleeve
1 in.
Lining cutting line

not necessary if you plan to dry-clean the garment. Otherwise, press the seams together and use a zigzag stitch or a machine or serger overlock stitch to finish the edges. Next, form the back pleat by stitching along the center back for 1 in. to 2 in. at the top, waist, and lower edge, being sure to lock in the stitch. Finally, staystitch the neckline.

Attaching the lining

Because there are many variations on how to attach the lining, here are some guidelines.

- Attach the lining to the neck trim or neck seam if there is a collar or hood.
- Attach the lining to the front ribbing on the grosgrain. The 1-in. seam allowance at the front edge will probably get used up when you pin the lining to the front edge depending on how much the sweater stretches. Adjust the seam allowance to suit the sweater knit, making sure there is enough ease in the lining.
- Attach the lining to the sleeve and bottom by connecting to the upper ribbing or upper hem. To do this, first press back the lining to be the same length as the finished sweater, then baste the lining in place. Try on the garment and adjust the length if necessary; the lining should not be drooping below or pulling up the sweater hem. Finally, cut away any extra lining and stitch.
- Leave the hems free hanging on long, droopy knits, or finish the sleeve hems separately by sewing a casing and inserting a narrow elastic (see "Finishing the sleeve lining hem" on the facing page).

You may be able to attach some or all of the lining to the sweater by machine depending on how the sweater is fashioned. For example, if the sweater has a grosgrain ribbon at the front opening, you can machine-sew the lining seamline to the edge of the ribbon with right sides facing.

You can also machine-sew if there is a serged or narrow raised seam at the neckline and

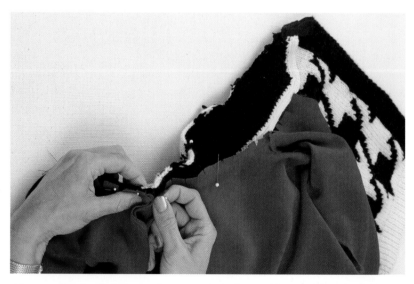

After sewing the lining together, staystitch the neckline. With right sides facing, pin the lining to the neck seam and front edges, then sew by machine.

ribbing. To do this, pin the lining seamline to the narrow seam with the right side of the lining facing the collar or the wrong side of the ribbing, then sew using a narrow zigzag stitch. Insert the lining using the bagged lining technique (see pp. 37-39). Leave an opening at one of the lining sleeves, then attach the lining to the neck seam and front edges first. Next, attach the lining and sleeve hems, then attach the lining at the bottom and close the sleeve opening.

If the lining is wider than the sweater near the ribbing, machine-sew a row of easestitching along the lining hemline to gather the lining. Turn back the lining hem allowance and slipstitch to the sweater ribbing.

Most full-fashion or hand-knit sweaters have a smooth transition between the ribbed trim and the body. On these garments, press under the seam allowance and slipstitch in place. If the lining is wider than the sweater at the bottom, use elastic thread to gather the bottom of the lining. Using elastic thread on the bobbin and all-purpose polyester thread on top, sew along the bottom lining seam with a long straight stitch with the right side of the lining facing up. Turn back the seam allowance and slipstitch to the top of the sweater ribbing.

Finishing the sleeve lining hem

To finish the sleeve hem, press back the hem ¼ in., then ⅝ in., and stitch close to the inner fold, leaving an opening near the side seam. Next, insert ¼-in. or ⅜-in.

Finish the sleeve lining hem by inserting elastic in the casing.

elastic into the casing and adjust the length of the elastic for comfort. Sew the elastic ends together and close the casing.

You can leave the sleeve lining disconnected from the sweater or hand-tack the lining hem to the top of the sleeve hem or ribbing at the side seam only.

10 Lining Vents

Vents can be found on all sorts of garments, including coats, skirts, dresses, and jackets. Even sleeves have vents. Vents are a classic detail that can be lined several ways. A classic vent (or kick pleat) and a French vent (or slit) look the same on the pattern but the difference is in the pressing. On the classic vent, both facings or extensions are pressed in the same direction to create a pleat or underlap. Pressing the facings or extensions away from the opening creates a French vent.

The vent area on all types of garments should be finished at the end of the construction process, in conjunction with hemming both the garment and the lining. Jacket linings must be connected to the vent and to the jacket hem to completely cover the inside layers. Coat, dress, and skirt vents may be connected to the lining but hemmed separately, or they can be hemmed separately at both the vent opening and hems. The easiest way to connect the lining to the vent underlap on all lining applications is to use a machine stitch and by stitching close to the edge.

In this chapter, I will show you how to make a lining pattern for a classic or French vent. I will then discuss how to sew a classic vent, a French vent, several versions of simplified vents, and a curved vent.

Making a Vent Lining Pattern

If a lining pattern is not provided, you can draw the lining adjustments onto the main garment pattern piece, thus eliminating the need to make a separate lining pattern. Before adjusting the pattern, it is important to allow for some ease above the vent area, otherwise you risk pulling on the outside layer when you wear the garment. If you finish sewing this area by hand, you can add some ease by sliding the lining up and misaligning the cut edges when connecting it to the vent area.

Changing the pattern makes it easier to finish the vent area either by hand or machine. This way the ease is built into the pattern and the cut edges will line up. Draw new pivot dots ½ in. below where they appear on the pattern and lower the cutting line by ½ in., then extend the back cutting line to meet this line (see the illustration at left). Mark the finished hem ½ in. lower at the center back and blend upward to the original hemline at the side seam. Next, mark the lining hem cutting line ⅝ in. below the new lining hemline. It's a good idea to mark these corrections in red or a contrasting color and use them as the reference points for marking the lining cutting lines on the garment pattern.

On the garment pattern, fold back the vent facing along the foldline so the facing is under the back pattern piece. Draw the cutting line 1¼ in. from the vent facing's edge. Label the new cutting line "Cutting line for left side" or overlap side (see the top illustration on the facing page).

When cutting the lining, it is easy to cut away the wrong side. For greater flexibility, cut both halves of the lining with the facing extensions and mark the new cutaway line and sewing line on *both* lining pieces using dressmaker carbon (see the bottom illustration on the facing page). If you are sewing a French vent, cut away both sides.

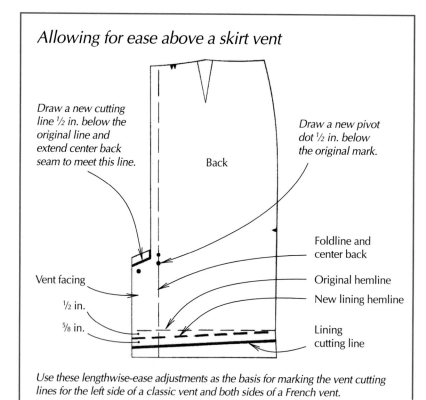

Allowing for ease above a skirt vent

Draw a new cutting line ½ in. below the original line and extend center back seam to meet this line.

Back

Draw a new pivot dot ½ in. below the original mark.

Vent facing

½ in.

⅝ in.

Foldline and center back

Original hemline

New lining hemline

Lining cutting line

Use these lengthwise-ease adjustments as the basis for marking the vent cutting lines for the left side of a classic vent and both sides of a French vent.

Marking vent cutting lines for left side of classic vent or both sides of French vent

Fold back the vent facing along the foldline so the facing is under the pattern.

Vent facing edge

1¼ in.

Lining hem cutting line

Lining cutting line for left side overlap of classic vent or for both sides of French vent

Marking vent cutting lines for both sides of classic vent

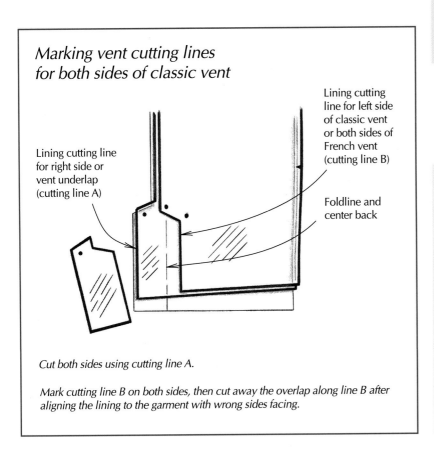

Lining cutting line for right side or vent underlap (cutting line A)

Lining cutting line for left side of classic vent or both sides of French vent (cutting line B)

Foldline and center back

Cut both sides using cutting line A.

Mark cutting line B on both sides, then cut away the overlap along line B after aligning the lining to the garment with wrong sides facing.

ALLOWING FOR LENGTHWISE EASE

Whenever you connect the lining to the outside vent, lengthwise ease is important to keep the lining from distorting the outer seam. If your garment pattern includes a lining pattern, it probably does not allow for lengthwise ease above the vent. You can check this by lining up the back garment and back lining patterns, matching the center back and upper edges. If the tops of the vents line up, there is no lengthwise ease above the vent. The illustration on the facing page shows how to allow for ease above the vent, and the illustration above left shows how to mark the cutting line for the left side, or overlap side, of the vent.

References to left and right in sewing directions refer to the garment or lining as it is worn on your body. On most standard lining applications you wear the lining with the wrong side facing out and the finished side facing the body, just the opposite of the garment. Identifying left or right side is critical when sewing asymmetric garments and asymmetric details such as a classic vent.

Sewing a Classic Vent

When sewing a classic vent, the garment is prepared first, then the lining. Finally, the lining can be attached to the vent after hemming the garment and the lining separately. When sewing skirts and dresses, you can use the alternate quick method, leaving the lining hanging completely free at the vent.

To prepare the garment vent, press under but don't stitch the ⅝-in. seam allowance on the right vent opening, which is the underlap. Using a small piece of fusible interfacing, reinforce the inside corner of the underlap.

Pin and sew the center back seam and upper vent, starting at the upper vent and pivoting on the dot at the inside corner. Next, clip the right vent to the corner diagonally and press the center back seam open above the vent, then press the left vent facing back along the center foldline. Press the right vent underlap toward the left side of the garment so it touches the left vent facing.

Next, cut out the garment lining, being sure to cut the vent using the outer vent cutting line and to mark the left vent cutting line on both vents so you won't cut away the wrong side. On the lining, sew the center back seam, stopping and backstitching at

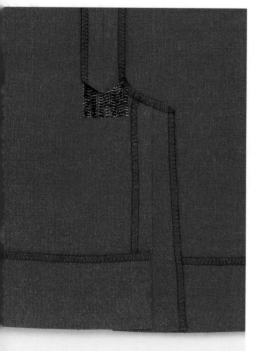

To prepare the garment, reinforce the inside corner of the right vent underlap with fusible interfacing and press back the right vent seam allowance.

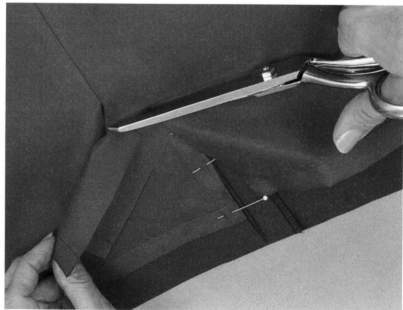

With the lining on top of the skirt and wrong sides facing, cut off the left back extension of the lining along the marked cutting line.

the dot, then press the seam open. Place the lining on top of the garment with wrong sides facing and cut away the left back extension, or overlap, along the new cutting line. Then reinforce-stitch the inside corner of the overlap along the sewing line and clip to the corner.

Press back the ⅝-in. seam allowance on the right vent opening, then clip to the corner where the center back seam ends and the top of the vent begins so you can press the underlap toward the overlap.

Sew the body of the lining together, then attach the lining to the garment and press back but don't sew the garment hem.

The vent facing should fold over the garment hem. Press the lower part of the vent facing again so that the folded edge has a sharp crease. To reduce bulk, trim the hem allowance beyond the foldline at the hem facing to ½ in., then press back and machine-stitch the lining hem so that it is 1 in. shorter than the garment.

The next step is to connect the the lining to the vent underlap. To do this, pin the garment underlap to the lining underlap with wrong sides facing, lining up the folded edges. Tuck the lining hem under the turned-up garment hem and edgestitch.

If you plan to hand-finish the vent, staystitch the entire sewing line, pivoting at the corner, to make it easier to press back the lining seam allowance.

Edgestitching is the easiest and quickest way to attach the lining to the garment at the vent underlap.

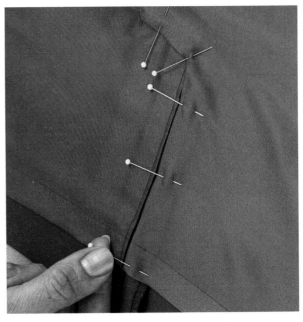

Fold under and pin the top and left side of the vent.

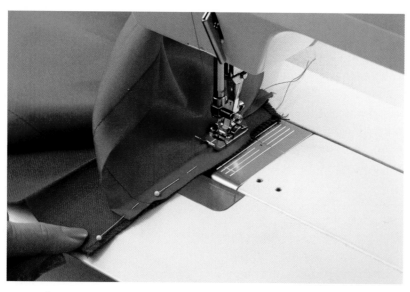

To machine-sew a classic vent, reach inside the skirt and pin the seam allowances together, then sew the lining to the vent facing.

Fold under and pin the top and left side of the vent, then hand-sew the folded edges using a slipstitch. You could also machine-sew by reaching between the layers and repinning the seam allowances with right sides facing. Machine-sew the lengthwise seam first, then sew the top of the vent. Finish hemming the garment, then use a small piece of fusible web or a slipstitch to hold the facing overlap in place on the garment hem.

Coat vents

Coat vents are sewn just like the classic vent. Begin by creating the vent lining pattern (see p. 136), or if your coat pattern includes a lining pattern, checking to see if there is lengthwise ease (see the tip on p. 137) and adjusting the lining pattern if necessary. As with a skirt or

dress, hem the coat and lining separately, making the lining length 1 in. shorter than the garment length before connecting the lining to the vent facings. Always connect the underlap by machine, then connect the lining to the overlap either by hand or by machine.

Jacket vents

Jacket vents are sewn the same as the classic vent except with a jacket you must connect the lining hem to the jacket hem and completely cover the inside layers.

Prepare the jacket vent area before installing the lining. Working from the wrong side of the jacket, press the left vent facing back along the center fold with a sharp crease. At the vent underlap, press back the ⅝-in. seam allowance along the lengthwise vent seam, then clip to the center back seam at the top of the vent underlap so that you can press the underlap toward the left vent. Press back and sew the jacket hem, being sure to fold the vent facing over the hem. To reduce bulk, trim the jacket hem allowance at the vent facing to ½ in. or miter the corner seam.

Next, cut out the jacket lining, remembering to cut the vent using the outer vent cutting line and to mark the left vent cutting line on both vents. Sew the lining together, then line up the wrong side of the lining to the wrong side of the jacket at the vent and cut away the left vent extension along the marked cutting line.

Finishing the vent with the modified hand method To prepare the lining for insertion using the modified hand method, staystitch the left vent seamline, pivoting at the inside corner. Clip to the corner and press back the seam allowance using the staystitching as a guide, and press back the ⅝-in. seam allowance on the vent underlap and at the lining hem.

When installing the lining, leave 4 in. unstitched at each front facing near the hem. Pin and slipstitch the lining hem to the top of the jacket hem, then pin the lining underlap to the jacket underlap, starting at the top of the vent and smoothing or finger-pressing the excess lining length toward the hem to form a pleat. Next, edgestitch with the jacket vent facing up and starting at the top of the vent.

Pin the left vent lining to the vent facing, starting at the top of the vent and again smoothing the excess length toward the hem to form a pleat. Slipstitch the lining edge to the vent facing. Finish the lower part of the vent facing the same way as the lower part of the front facings by using a hand whipstitch, a machine or serger overlock stitch, or by binding the edge with a Hong

Kong finish. If using an overlock stitch or a Hong Kong finish, also use fusible web to hold the facing in place.

Finishing the vent when bagging the lining To machine-finish a jacket vent when bagging the lining, the sewing order is changed so you can turn the jacket right side out through the vent underlap instead of through the sleeve opening.

After sewing the lining together, reinforce-stitch the inside corner of the left vent and clip to the corner. Press back the ⅝-in. seam allowance at the right vent underlap. Attach the lining to the jacket, folding up the raw edges of the lining hem to line up with the raw edges of the jacket hem at the front facings. Line up and baste the top of the right lining vent to the top of the right jacket vent with wrong sides facing. Pin the left vent lining to the left vent facing with right sides facing, folding up the raw edges of the lining hem to line up with the raw edges of the jacket hem. Next, machine-stitch, pivoting at the corner.

Reach between the layers to pin and sew the left lining hem to the jacket hem with right sides facing, getting as close as possible to the front facing and the vent facing. Turn right side out, press a soft crease at the lining hem, and use a small piece of fusible web to hold the vent facing in place at the jacket hem.

On coat and jacket linings, press the center back seam, center back pleat, and vent underlap toward the left back lining. Doing so eliminates the need to clip the lining seam allowance at the top of the vent.

Next, reach through the vent underlap to pin and sew the remaining lining hem to the jacket hem with right sides facing, getting as close as possible to the front facing. Pin and edgestitch the vent underlap to the lining, then press a soft crease at the lining hem.

Sleeve vents

Technically, you can line the sleeve vents the same way you line a classic vent, as is often done on couture garments. But since the sleeve vents have no function, it is more efficient to eliminate the vent adjustment on the sleeve lining.

To do this, eliminate the extensions when you cut the lining. At the sleeve vent, adjust the upper and under sleeve patterns by marking the lining cutting line ⅝ in. from the vent foldline. Also mark the sleeve cutting line ⅝ in. below the finished hemline. Sew the seams as you would standard seams, then attach the lining hem to the sleeve hem by hand or by machine. The lining will cover up the back side of the sleeve vent.

Sewing a French Vent

With a French vent, both sides of the vent are the same so both sides of the vent lining adjustment are also the same. To adjust a lining pattern, allow for ease above the vent (see the illustration on p. 136), and mark the cutting line for both sides of the French vent. The cutting line is the same adjustment as for the left side on a classic vent (see the top illustration on p. 137).

Prepare the garment vents by pressing back the right and left vent facings along the center foldline. Next, press back the garment hem, fold the vent facings over the hem, and press the lower part of the vent again to form a sharp crease at the edge. To reduce bulk, trim the hem allowance beyond the foldlines at both hem facings to ½ in.

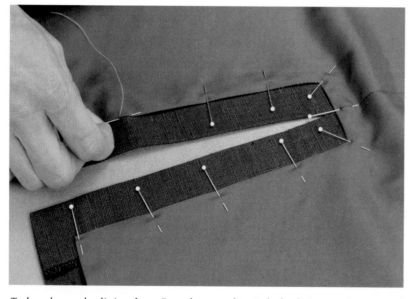

To hand-sew the lining for a French vent, slipstitch the lining to the top and sides of the vent facings.

Cut and sew the lining body. Sew the vent seam, starting at

the dot that marks the vent opening and locking in the stitch. Reinforce-stitch the inside corner of the left and right vent. Next, attach the lining to the garment, and hem the lining so that it is 1 in. shorter than the garment. Clip to the corners, then press the lining under along the stitching line, pin to the garment vent, and hand-finish the folded edge using a slipstitch. If you machine-sew, reach between the layers and repin the lining and vent seam allowances with right sides facing, aligning the cut edges. Machine-sew each side, pivoting at the corner.

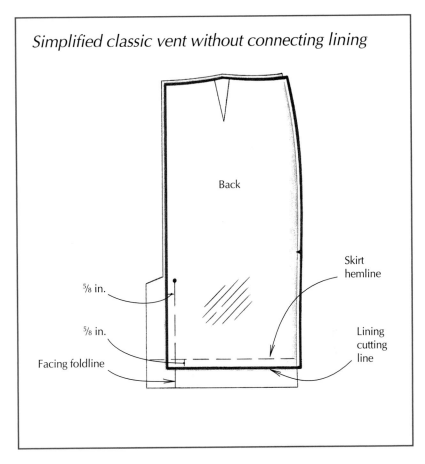

Simplified classic vent without connecting lining

Back

Skirt hemline

Lining cutting line

⅝ in.

⅝ in.

Facing foldline

Simplified Vents

While I prefer the classic lining application on tailored jackets and coats, quick finishes have their place. Simplified techniques are perfect for dresses and skirts because they are easier and faster to do. You can also use the simplified techniques on jackets and coats that have simple shapes and a relaxed fit, such as all types of ethnic, craft-inspired, or wearable-art garments.

Simplified classic vent

An easy way to finish the classic vent on a skirt or dress is by leaving a ⅝-in. seam allowance at the lining vent instead of making the pattern changes for the left and right sides of the vent (see the illustration above). There is no need to allow for

lengthwise ease because the lining is not connected to the vent. Finishing these edges is easy, as you just press back the seam allowance twice and stitch in place to form a slit.

To use this technique, prepare the garment vent in the same way as the classic vent. You should also finish the raw edges using a zigzag stitch or a machine or serger overlock stitch because the lining does not connect to the garment vent.

Press back but don't sew the garment hem, and fold the vent

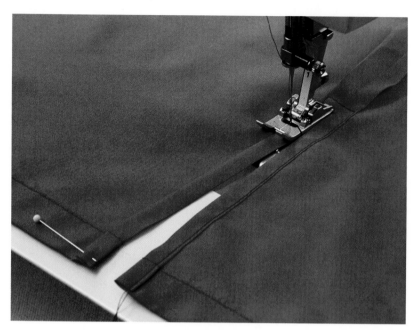

For a simplified classic vent, turn under and sew the seam allowances, pivoting at the top of the vent.

Simplified French vent

Here are three other ways to finish the French vent that are simpler to cut and sew. For the first two variations, cut both the garment and the lining vents with a ⅝-in. seam allowance and lower the vent opening dot by ½ in. on the lining only to allow for lengthwise ease. Also lower the hem cutting line ½ in. at the center back and blend to the original line at the side seam (see the illustration on the facing page). For the third variation, the garment pattern is unchanged, but you hem the lining vent separately from the garment after cutting the lining at an angle so that it does not show when you walk.

For the first variation, sew the vent seam on both the garment and the lining, starting at the dot that marks the vent opening and being sure to lock in the stitch. On the garment, press back the seam allowances along the vent, then press up and sew the garment hem, making sure the folded ends line up at the vent. After hemming the lining to be 1 in. shorter than the garment, press back the seam allowances along the vent.

To finish, pin the garment and lining vents with wrong sides facing and edgestitch with the garment on top. Sew with a continuous seam, going up one side of the vent, pivoting at the top, and going down the other.

facing over the garment hem. To reduce bulk, trim the hem allowance beyond the foldline at the hem facing to ½ in. Hem the garment and use a small piece of fusible web or a slipstitch to hold the facing overlap in place on the garment hem. Next, machine-stitch the edge of the vent underlap using a ⅛-in. or ¼-in. seam allowance to hold the pressed-back seam in place. Press back and machine-stitch the lining hem so that it is 1 in. shorter than the garment.

Finish the raw edges along the lining vent by pressing under the seam allowance, then folding the raw edges in to the foldline and pressing again. Stitch using a continuous ¼-in. seam allowance, starting at the hem, pivoting at the top of the vent, and ending at the hem.

For the second method, in which the lining is sewed to the vent invisibly, mark but don't sew the garment hemline near the vent, then hem the lining to be 1 in. shorter than the garment. Connect the lining to each side of the vent by pinning and stitching the lining vent seam to the garment vent seam with right sides facing. Sew each vent seam individually, starting near the top of the vent and ending at the lining hem.

It is a good idea to have a small gap of about ¼ in. at the top of the vent where the vent seam meets the garment seam because when the seams meet or the stitches overlap, the outside of the garment will pucker. At each vent seam, fold up the garment hem along the hemline with right sides facing and sew the bottom of the vent seam again, catching the garment hem. Trim or grade the vent seam depending on the thickness of the fabrics you are using, and trim the corners diagonally. Turn the vent right side out and press the vent seam flat, then finish hemming the garment.

By using the third method, you can finish the French vent without connecting the lining if you cut the lining diagonally at the vent opening. To do this, you need to mark the lining vent cutting line directly on the garment pattern. Begin by folding the vent facing along the foldline and marking a dot where

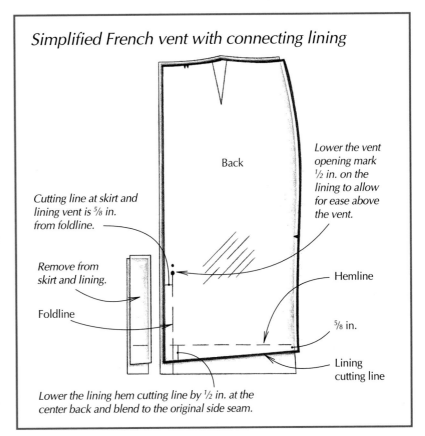

Simplified French vent with connecting lining

Back

Lower the vent opening mark ½ in. on the lining to allow for ease above the vent.

Cutting line at skirt and lining vent is ⅝ in. from foldline.

Remove from skirt and lining.

Foldline

Hemline

⅝ in.

Lining cutting line

Lower the lining hem cutting line by ½ in. at the center back and blend to the original side seam.

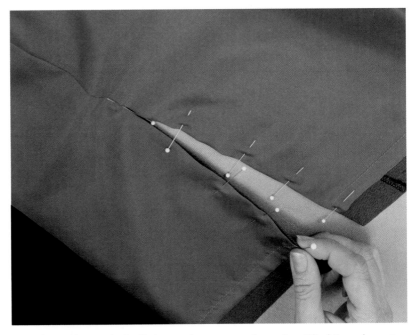

Pin, then edgestitch the lining to the garment for a simplified French vent, being sure to sew with the garment on top.

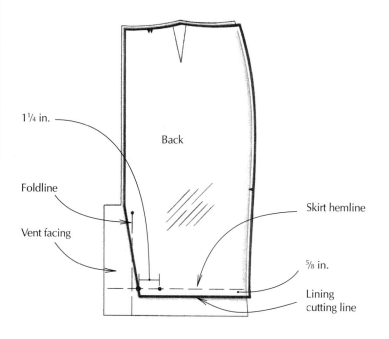

Simplified French vent without connecting lining

1¼ in.

Back

Foldline

Vent facing

Skirt hemline

⅝ in.

Lining
cutting line

Fold the vent facing along the foldline and mark a dot where the facing's outer edge crosses the skirt's hemline. Mark a second dot 1¼ in. from the first dot in the direction of the facing, then draw the vent cutting line by connecting the second dot to the cutting line at the top of the vent.

using a zigzag stitch or a machine or serger overlock stitch. Next, hem the garment and connect the lower facing edges to the hem using a slipstitch or a small piece of fusible web.

Hem the lining to be 1 in. shorter than the garment. Trim any part of the lining hem that extends beyond the vent cutting line. At the lining vent, press under the ⅝-in. seam allowance, then fold and press the cut edge into the foldline. Stitch using a continuous ¼-in. seam allowance, starting at the hem, pivoting at the top of the vent, and ending at the hem.

Curved Vents

Vents and front facings with graceful outside curves also have curved inner facing edges. You find these details on jackets, vests, tunics, coats, and occasionally on dresses and skirts with curved lower edges or shirttail vents at the side seams.

To facilitate lining garments that have curved vents and facings without changing the actual garments, you should square the inner facing curves, then use the adjusted facings and the garment pattern to create the lining pattern. It is much easier to attach the lining to the garment when you square the inside curves, particularly on jackets and vests, because you will want to connect the lining at the hem.

the facing's edge crosses the garment hemline (see the illustration above). Unfold the pattern, and mark a second dot 1¼ in. in the direction of the facing, then connect this dot to the garment cutting line above the vent. This diagonal line is the lining vent cutting line.

To finish the vent area on the garment, press back the vent facings and hem the garment. The vent facings always fold over the hem. Finish the vent edges

Squaring the inner facing curves can be done in one of two ways. With the first method, you square the inner curved edges where the vent facing curves into the hem facing. To do this, mark the new inner edge by extending the vertical and horizontal edges using a ruler so the edges intersect, thus creating an inside corner. You could also use a triangle or an L-square to square the corner. Cut the facings with the lengthwise grain going across the hem to stabilize the curved vents.

To create the lining pattern, place the adjusted facing pattern under the garment pattern, aligning the outer edges. Mark the lining cutting line 1¼ in. beyond the front facing, back facing, and vertical vent facing's inner edge (see the illustration on p. 148). To add ½ in. lengthwise ease above the vent opening, mark the cutting line 1¾ in. beyond the vent facing's upper edge. Cut the lining cutting length the same as the garment, and add a back pleat when you cut the lining by placing the center fold 1 in. from the folded lining fabric.

The second method of squaring curves involves squaring the facing at the top of the vent, which simplifies cutting and sewing the lining because there is no need to make any vent adjustments.

Because this lining is cut diagonally at the vent opening, it doesn't have to be sewn down, as it will not show through the skirt vent.

To use this method, square the hem facing by connecting the upper edges of the vent facings using a ruler or straight edge. Tape blank pattern paper to the facings in order to make this adjustment. When the pattern back or front are cut on the fold, extend the top vent cutting line to the center fold. Also extend the center foldline so it meets the new vent cutting line.

If the garment front has a front facing, extend the top vent cutting line to the front facing. Doing this creates a large facing at the bottom and places the lining hem at the top of the vents, thus completely bypassing the vents. Be sure to cut the facing with the lengthwise grain going across the bottom to stabilize the vents and keep them curving toward the body.

To create the lining pattern, place the adjusted facing pattern under the garment pattern and

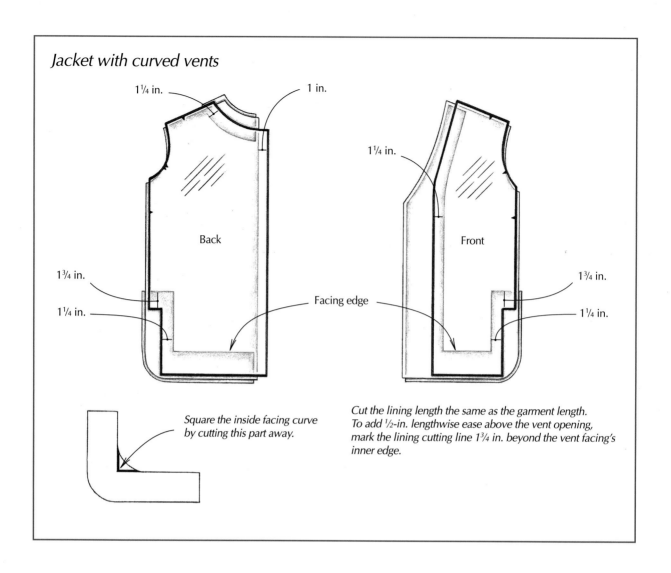

Jacket with curved vents

1¼ in.

1 in.

Back

1¾ in.

1¼ in.

Facing edge

1¼ in.

1¾ in.

1¼ in.

Front

Square the inside facing curve by cutting this part away.

Cut the lining length the same as the garment length. To add ½-in. lengthwise ease above the vent opening, mark the lining cutting line 1¾ in. beyond the vent facing's inner edge.

mark the lining cutting line 2½ in. beyond the facing's inner edge (see the illustration on the facing page). At the front and back neck facing, mark the lining cutting line 1¼ in. from the inner facing edge. When cutting the lining, add a back pleat by placing the center fold 1 in. from the folded lining fabric.

To sew curved vents on jackets, follow the directions for finishing the left vent using the modified hand method or the bagged lining technique (see pp. 141-142). If you are sewing curved vents on dresses, skirts, tunics, or coats with a free-hanging hem, follow the directions for finishing the French vent (see pp. 142-143).

Jacket with simplified curved vents

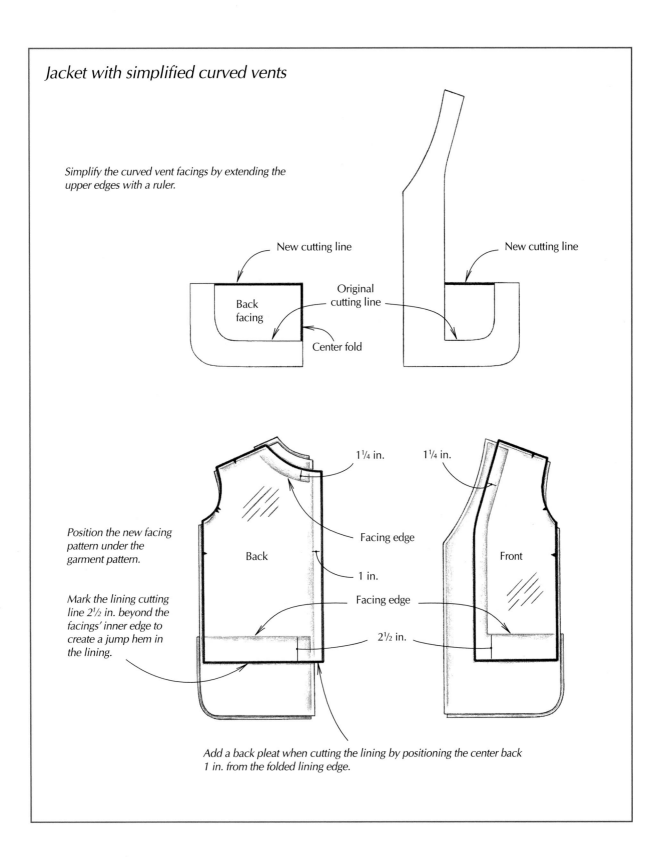

Simplify the curved vent facings by extending the upper edges with a ruler.

New cutting line

New cutting line

Original cutting line

Back facing

Center fold

1¼ in.

1¼ in.

Position the new facing pattern under the garment pattern.

Mark the lining cutting line 2½ in. beyond the facings' inner edge to create a jump hem in the lining.

Back

Facing edge

1 in.

Facing edge

Front

2½ in.

Add a back pleat when cutting the lining by positioning the center back 1 in. from the folded lining edge.

Sources

Apparel Component Supply/A.C.S.
447 West 36th St.
New York, NY 10018
Phone: (800) 739-8783
Fax: (212) 947-9281

Tailoring supplies, including coat lining materials, pattern tissue, and extra-long zippers. Catalog available.

Baer Fabrics
515 E. Market St.
Louisville, KY 40202
Phone: (502) 569-7010; (800) 769-7776
Fax: (502) 582-2331

Tailoring supplies and fabric, including Bemberg rayon. Catalog available.

Banksville Designer Fabrics
115 New Canaan Ave.
Norwalk, CT 06850
Phone: (203) 846-1333

Mail-order fabrics, including Bemberg rayon.

Britex
146 Geary St.
San Francisco, CA 94108
Phone: (415) 392-2910

Retail store and mail-order fabrics, trims, and buttons.

Dressmakers Supply
1212 Yonge St.
Toronto, ON, Canada M4T 1W1
Phone: (416) 922-6000

Sewing supplies, including notions, buttons, lining fabrics, coat linings, and pattern tissue.

A. Feibusch Corp.
27 Allen St.
New York, NY 10002
Phone: (212) 226-3964

Stocks zippers of every size, color, type, and application. Zippers made to order. Will answer written inquiries with SASE.

Foxglove Fabric Finders
112-346 Dunbar St.
Vancouver, BC, Canada V6S 2C2
Phone: (800) 607-2202

Mail-order fabric club. Carries hundreds of fabrics, including polyester and rayon linings. Canadian residents only.

G Street Mail-Order Services
12240 Wilkins Ave.
Rockville, MD 20852
Phone: (800) 333-9191

Offers quality fabrics, notions, lining fabrics, trims, and accessories and swatching service.

Grasshopper Hill Fabrics
4 Cataraqui St., Suite 306
Kingston, ON, Canada K7K 1Z7
Phone: (613) 548-3889; (800) 361-8275

Mail-order fabric source.

HE-RO Sewing Center
495 S. Clinton Ave.
Rochester, NY 14620
Phone: (716) 232-2160; (800) 739-9464

Tailoring supplies, including pocketing, Bemberg rayon, zippers, coat linings, and pattern tissue. Catalog available.

Oregon Tailor Supply Co.
2123 S.E. Division St.
P.O. Box 42284
Portland, OR 97242
Phone: (503) 232-6191; (800) 678-2457
Fax: (503) 232-9470

Sewing, tailoring, and dressmaking supplies and trims, including extra-long zippers and lining fabrics. Catalog available.

The Perfect Notion
Box 602
7620 Elbow Dr. SW
Calgary, AB, Canada T2B 1K2
Phone: (888) 999-8821

Sewing and quilting notions, Bemberg rayon, coat linings, and pattern tissue. Free catalog.

Sawyer Brook Distinctive Fabrics
P.O. Box 1800
Clinton, MA 01510-0813
Phone: (508) 368-3133; (800) 290-2739

Mail-order fabrics, including Bemberg rayon.

Vogue Fabrics by Mail
618 Hartrey Ave.
Evanston, IL 60202
Phone: (847) 864-1270; (800) 433-4313

Mail-order fabric club.

Wawak Corporation
2235 Hammond Dr.
Schaumburg, IL 60173
Phone: (847) 397-4850; (800) 654-2235

Tailoring supplies, linings, extra-long zippers, and buttons. Catalog available.

Index

Look for these and other *Threads* books at your local bookstore or sewing retailer.

Easy Guide to Serging Fine Fabrics

Easy Guide to Sewing Blouses

Easy Guide to Sewing Jackets

Easy Guide to Sewing Pants

Easy Guide to Sewing Skirts

Just Pockets

Sew the New Fleece

The Sewing Machine Guide

Fine Machine Sewing

50 Heirloom Buttons to Make

Couture Sewing Techniques

Shirtmaking

Beyond the Pattern

Distinctive Details

Fit and Fabric

Fitting Solutions

Fitting Your Figure

Great Quilting Techniques

Great Sewn Clothes

Jackets, Coats and Suits

Quilts and Quilting

Sewing Tips & Trade Secrets

Stitchery and Needle Lace

Techniques for Casual Clothes

For a catalog of the complete line of *Threads* books and videos, write to The Taunton Press, P.O. Box 5506, Newtown, CT 06470-5506.